Malachi Whitaker (1895–1975) w
grew up among books: her fath
hours in his workrooms reading
writing early but was savagely s
books of stories (a critic dubbed
1939, *And So Did I*. In the last thirty-six years of her life she wrote nothing more for publication. After the war her work fell into neglect. It was rediscovered in Joan Hart's 1984 selection, *The Crystal Fountain and Other Stories*, and since then her stories have been widely anthologised and broadcast.

MALACHI WHITAKER

And So Did I

PALADIN
GRAFTON BOOKS
A Division of the Collins Publishing Group

LONDON GLASGOW
TORONTO SYDNEY AUCKLAND

Paladin
Grafton Books
A Division of the Collins Publishing Group
8 Grafton Street, London W1X 3LA

Published in Paladin Books 1990

First published in Great Britain by
Carcanet Press Limited 1987

ISBN 0-586-08755-9

Printed and bound in Great Britain by
Collins, Glasgow

Set in Bembo

And a thousand thousand slimy things
Lived on; and so did I.

Ancient Mariner

AND SO DID I

Yesterday, I saw an accident. A man was standing on an island in the middle of the road, and a car swept by, taking him with it on the bonnet. For perhaps half a second he stuck there, then he was flung into the road with a heavy, smacking sound. He jumped up and staggered back to the island, to the friends from whom he had been torn, out of the way of coming traffic which he seemed to feel already rolling carelessly over his legs. People held him, and his hat fell off, slowly. He lifted it up, and put it tremblingly back on his head with both hands. The car had stopped, inert. On the near side, a door opened, and two long woman's legs hung out of it, then were drawn up again. There did not seem to be a policeman in this renowned London square. People drifted lightly about. The man was taken across to a bar. There had been a shower, and soon the traffic was moving along with that sticky, tearing sound it has after rain. But the car that had been the cause of the trouble still lolled there, heavy and stupid, as if to say, 'This might be forgotten, it might be forgotten, I might have done no harm at all'.

Later in the evening, my husband and I were strolling along a quiet street. He was taking me home, because we were staying in different places. We stopped to kiss good-night, and a superfluous, rubber-tipped policeman flashed a light in our faces. I could have spat at him, but I had no spit.

Now I am in my northern home again. The children are

in bed, and my mind is as pure as snow — perhaps the result of eating a great deal of fruit? Whatever the reason is, I feel astonishingly clean, and have been reading St Paul's Epistles to the Romans, the Corinthians, the Galatians, the Ephesians, and so on, as long as my eyes could see.

For at last, I have time to take up my long-abandoned search for God and the Truth. But my mind will keep going back to a box of peaches which I had sent to me when I was in a nursing home five months ago. Each peach eventually sank into a different stomach. But before they were eaten, their perfection of look was imprinted on my mind. The God I was brought up on was the one which Blake drew floating on beard and cloud. Each peach reminded me of Blake's particular God. Now, God and the peaches and the delicate niceness of the girl who sent them to me are inextricably mixed together and will not come apart.

The truth is not yet in me, but it may come. I never give up hope. In any case, we have recently bought a darts board, and it is surprising to me how much fun there is in a game of darts. Shove-ha'penny is too earnest, and you have to play knur-and-spell — a local game — outside. But the rules of darts are clear and good. Each player does his own work, and needs neither caddie nor instructor. Beginners have as much chance as anybody. They seem to bathe in pools of luck the first game, and that encourages them. I could wish that Gray had put an immortal line about darts in his Elegy.

Gratitude is a surprising thing. I have just read a Victorian novel called *Not Wisely but Too Well*, by Rhoda Broughton. My father said to me not long ago, 'What? Have you never read anything of Miss Broughton's?'

(It might have been Miss Braddon's or even Miss Emma Jane Worboise's — these names come sailing up out of the past.) In this novel a very young and rather peculiar female, who nearly comes to life in two or three places, is asked by a tall, dark, sinister, powerful and fearfully loved middle-aged man to elope with him. It took a hundred and eleven pages of very small print for them to come to their first kiss — but what a kiss it was! 'And off went the last rag of restraint, and he wrapped his arms around her as she stood before him, tighter, tighter, and bent down his head from its stately height, to her small, uplifted face, nearer, nearer, till their lips met and were joined in a wedlock so fast, so long enduring, so firm, that it seemed as if they could never be divorced again.' I was breathless myself before I got to the end of this description.

The young woman, whose name is Kate, is not warned that he is married until one evening, when she is sitting with Dare (an ideal hero-villain's name) on 'a heap of stones'. Surely the wrong place to tell her, when she is probably worrying inwardly about her cold bottom, that he is already married.

As soon as she understands, ' "Married!" said Kate at last, in a voice like an old man's.' In less than no time she is calling him Colonel Stamer. He admits that he has been so sure of her that he has a groom waiting with a dogcart at the corner of the lane.

But if Dare had been the young man Miss Broughton really meant him to be, why should he sit his young woman on a heap of stones to tell her he was married? What was to stop him — after that kiss — from making violent and satisfactory love to her, and then bundling her into the dogcart? Does 'the public' really want to be led up the garden and then dragged in to religion and good works and poor parsons and death? I say 'does' and not 'did', because the whole book is a monument of sincerity, and if it were re-written in the jargon of today, would probably be as good a seller as ever.

No, it is all as garbled as the way I have got mixed up in sincerity and gratitude, and will not disentangle myself. At the moment I'm out for pleasure. And I remember this bit of the novel with deep pleasure.

' "Let's sit down and rest," said Dare. "It's awfully nice on the grass in this bit of shade." '

It *was* 'awfully nice'; but was it 'awfully' wholesome? I think not.'

In the end, he is run over by his own dogcart, and dies with his head in Kate's lap. She doesn't do much to comfort him. She says, 'Oh, my poor, dear fellow, you *are* going somewhere indeed! Oh, I wonder if it is anywhere good?'

It is very evident that Miss Broughton had a strict and strong idea of sin as Sin, which seems to have passed me by. She knew sin and not gratitude, whereas it is the other way round with me.

Last night (for it is another day now) when I was reading the Bible, in search of truth, I came upon the following well-known passage, which struck me in a new manner:

'And Saul, yet breathing out threatenings and slaughter against the disciples of the Lord, went unto the high priest.

'And desired of him letters to Damascus to the synagogues, that if he found any of this way, whether they were men or women, he might bring them bound into Jerusalem.

'And as he journeyed, he came near Damascus: and suddenly there shined round about him a light from heaven:

'And he fell to the earth, and heard a voice saying unto him, Saul, Saul, why persecutest thou me?

'And he said, Who art thou, Lord? And the Lord said, I am Jesus whom thou persecutest: it is hard for thee to kick against the pricks.

'And he trembling and astonished said, Lord, what wilt thou have me to do? And the Lord said unto him, Arise, and go into the city, and it shall be told thee what thou must do.'

Lucky, lucky Saul! First, because he was so incensed against the Christians that he wanted authority to go about rounding them up, and second, because when he was doing it, there 'shined round about him a light from heaven'. Only think, millions and millions of us, in every nation and place, can go from cradle to grave without an active desire to persecute anybody. So a light from heaven will never shine about us, and no soft, sad voice will say 'Why persecutest thou me?'

And there's a third thing, and that's the way he was told to go into the city, 'and it shall be told thee what thou must do'. Yes, lucky, lucky Saul, to have all responsibility taken from him! All that was left for him was to do as he was told, then he could be sure of eternal salvation.

I can only sigh and pass on, because the Hound of Heaven and me seem to keep about the same distance apart, both lolloping along with our tongues out, downhill, and stopping at the same time for meals and so forth. I have never even felt his warm breath at my shoulder.

Sometimes I am appalled when I realize how very ignorant I am. I like reading, but I have never studied anything. I can see things in flashes, but cannot draw learned conclusions from them. There are people who can sit on the reading room at the British Museum, quietly sucking imaginary marrow out of dead bones for hours on end, and feathering their nests with it. They fill me with real awe. They are the Sauls of Great Russell Street. A voice has come to them saying, Arise and go into the city, and it shall be told thee what thou must do.

And they do it, by God, they do it! That is why we get so much twice and thrice and ten times cooked stuff to feed our souls. Who is looking for truth, and who is looking for money? And now I could wish I had learned to think, for the subject swells too much, and has to be kicked away to make room for another. After all, life is a dream of sorts, the kind of dream in which you can't pack a dozen people into four single beds to sleep.

Yesterday, I was reading the story of Noel Coward's life, written by himself, giving his point of view. Somewhere in the world there are bits of happiness, but not in this book. There is the feeling that he is always trying to find what other people are thinking, but either doesn't know or won't say what he thinks himself. He is growing older, he has had some noisy successes and failures simply told, he has been driven by the demon of work, but not yet by the angel. I have not met him. I have only seen him once or twice far away upon a stage, acting, talking quietly to Gertrude Lawrence most of the time. (This didn't seem fair, because Gertrude Lawrence must know all his words by now, and many people in the audience wouldn't. I didn't. I must buy his plays and read them some time, if life lasts so long.)

I keep on thinking of the small boy Noel Coward, who was asked to sing, and stood up and did. Like that. But I prefer a small, forgotten girl of seven I once saw, egged on to recite by her mother. This child lifted her dress over the back of her head in a kind of trance, put her foot through the glass of a bookcase door, was suddenly filled with intense pity for the listening world, shouted 'No!' in a tremendous voice, and fled. She may never amount to anything, but she had one moment of understanding in this life.

Yet I liked the book! I was entranced by it! I sat the whole day in my dressing-gown, just reading and enjoying it. The man knows more about himself than anybody. And he can write. Yet the impression he gives is one of a human being just functioning. You can wait for the heights. You can wait for the depths. Yes, you can wait.

It is strange to know people who have written books, and so on; people who have seen things, and sat down, and made a kind of twisted spiral of smoke out of their thoughts. For that is how it is. Nothing can last in this transient world much longer than a plume of smoke. I am not saying this because I am forty-two this year, I have thought it ever since I could put half a dozen words together, or knew of death. Yet the first large dead thing I saw was a cat in a gutter, when I was twenty-one. But long before that, I knew how the sky itself changed in the moment of looking at it, and how even a blade of grass in high pride withered before the midday sun.

It is a pity that some people have to grow old. I felt this, because I got a letter from a friend, a writer, last Monday, saying that he was passing near, and could he stay the night? He could, and did. And how quickly that time passed. He was to take a six-weeks' walking holiday in the north, in the dales and the Lake district, and was dressed in comfortable though not noticeable light clothes. He had enough love of colour to wear a pink shirt and a blue tie.

I am sure this man will find a certain amount of happiness walking from dale to dale and lake to lake in six weeks. He is rather more like a lone animal than a man. I have heard echoes of his human past from other people, but he doesn't carry the burden of it about with him. But there is the consciousness of his connection with humanity in the sudden glow of fire in his dark eye. I think he does not want to grow old, or to die. I should think that when he is dying, he will make terrific efforts to come back to this earth. His eyes will flash and pale, flash and pale, until suddenly they can darken no more with this secret life he keeps inside himself, and what he has of spirit will be gone. God *might* make exceptions in favour of these people who want to live for ever, and make them live, say, for four or five hundred years.

It is strange how the children will hang round me as soon as they see I am writing. At half-past eleven, Nicholas is still in his dressing-gown — simply because I am, I suppose. We shared a biscuit at eleven. He has been reading *Everybody's Weekly*, a twopenny journal which arrives at this house every Monday, and has a very peculiar smell, due either to the printing ink, or to the fact that it is kept near strong fire-lighters at some point in its journey.

I like *Everybody's Weekly*. It seems to fill a definite need. Surely there are times when most of us want to read some straightforward, thrilling fact, such as 'She Boiled Fly-papers — and Became Mass Murderess', or 'Only Had Penknife, but Fought Man-eating Tiger', or even 'He Exhibited a Red Nose at the Flower Show!' These are headings. But again, if there is time enough in this life, I will read what is beneath them, perhaps with the same serious intensity as does my seven-year-old adopted son.

We keep fires all summer in this cold northern house. Ah, but it is warm here in winter, and our winter lasts for nine months. I have my rooms in the new part, which was run up in front of the old house in sixteen hundred and twenty-seven. We are supposed to dine in the old part, built who knows when, in a room twenty-four feet long, held up by heavy oak beams, and floored in stone flags. But I have most of my meals brought in here on a tray, in here, where there is a thick carpet with two layers of felt underneath it, and where the chairs and divans are comfortable and very soft, where the colours of things blend softly too, and where muffled music continually decants itself out of a mock-walnut box into the bottle of my soul (or could I say amphora, with thanks to Roget's *Thesaurus*, though this is the first time it has given me a good answer. I keep it for the sake of my literary friends, those who cannot live without it).

I love these bangings and knockings which come out of the wireless box, or radiogramophone (for it has a high-sounding name of some kind), these sawings of a cello in two, these drawn-out raspings of over-rated fiddles. And I love to be able to stop the noise of suddenly screaming sopranos. Ah, to hear that row coming out of the sound-amplifier, to bear it in agony, and then to crack on the bliss of silence, and tremble with peace!

One day last week, feeling lazy and yet critical, I switched on the radio, and sat down to listen to it for hours. Men and women bawled shamelessly to heaven all day for Love, Luv, Larve and Lurve. One would have thought they had plenty of everything else, soap, and food, and dandelions, and needed nothing but *that* to make this earth a paradise. Announcers giving out the titles of gramophone records in their charmingly toned yet expressionless voices asked the same thing of heaven. It must have been a kind of Love Day, or so an astonished god would have thought.

Today, a woman I know has become a grandmother. She did not tell me — I saw the announcement of the birth of a child to her daughter-in-law in the local paper. I asked her if it was so, as she had not mentioned the imminence of the event. And she was filled with shame because the child was a girl.

'We're all so disappointed,' she said. 'Everything seemed to point to its being a boy. Even the doctor thought so.'

This point of view leaves me breathless. For twenty years I have been hoping — and with my disposition this means trying hard — to produce an infant of one sex or another. But I cannot manage to do it. No chemist knows me except as a buyer of toothbrushes and toilet rolls. I do not become pale and ill with worry every few weeks as many of my women friends do. On the whole, I bear my cross of barrenness easily now, because I have learned that it is much the easier one to bear than the cross of fertility, which *is* a cross in these particular days.

I have been pitched from doctor to doctor — even landing once in Harley Street — without any result to date beyond a few operations, which I found truly comic, and which I survived with healthy optimism. I do things too quickly. When I begin to write a story, I know I must finish it before I rest. There are odd stops for meals, but no real break. I am driven before too strong a gale. Perhaps there isn't enough patience in me to make a baby in the regulation time, and the one who thought the thing out isn't going to alter the design for my sake. So I remain a barren woman, which is a reproach to me. Excuse me.

Something had to be done about it. There's always a next best thing, and sometimes it turns out to be the best thing after all. I have adopted two children, a girl and a boy, and after some years of their company and affection and devilment, I have come to the conclusion that I could never have produced two such utterly satisfactory children myself. And when they do something awful, I can't turn to my husband and say scathingly, 'There, that's *your* family coming out'.

We had thought of adoption several times, and like many other people, knew nothing about it. I really wanted to start with a new-born baby, but supposed I should have to begin with quite an old child. I was so simple as to believe that nobody could possibly part with a thing so helpless and small. A friend of mine who was without money or husband found that in spite of these facts she was going to have a baby. She set off, and walked a long, long way to a workhouse, and got her baby, and stuck to it. For a long time, she had to do a lot of work — floor-scrubbing, and washing old pauper-women — things she had never done in her life before. But eventually she got a job as housekeeper to a working man, where a child was 'not objected to'. And there she is. She has made a life for herself.

However, lots of people want to dump their children. But some poor little ones are left orphans through no fault of their own. And though we had decided very solemnly that we would care not a jot for family history, we found ourselves the adoptive parents of a child with an eminently satisfactory lineage, and one much more gentle than our own. There are traces of breeding in him which we don't possess, but which we can respect and admire, though he is no cuckoo in the nest.

This takes me back to the day, nearly seven years ago, when I went to the National Adoption Society's office in Baker Street, and asked just how one adopted a child. I can see the doorway yet, and those strange steps of clean, green linoleum, and the stern face of a young employee who thought I was an Erring, and not a Virtuous expectant mother.

This all led to the Harlesden Jubilee Clock. It became very well known to me, this clock, because it is very near Acton Road, and a walk of a minute along Acton Road brought me to the society's Baby Hostel. This house stands alone in a pleasant garden. I could see the trees over a black, wooden fence, and I still remember the look of them on that still, June day, and the feel of the hot sun through my thin clothes. I suppose I was having my last day of a sort of freedom.

There's a high gate with a small notice on it. I went into the garden for the first time with the feeling that my stomach had got into my neck. For something told me that my fate was in there, and that there was plenty of hard work attached to it. There were a lot of cots with peaceful infants in them spread along a veranda. They had been recently fed, and that makes a difference to any of us.

I rang a bell, and peeped into the cots at the same time. Lover as I am, these children looked more or less alike to me, flabby yet tanned, most of them with dark circles beneath their eyes. These were the very young. They squirmed, and snorted, and twisted their lips in their sleep, and moved their bald or slightly hairy heads upon immaculate pillows.

The matron showed me round herself. She was dressed in brown, and wore a frilled white bonnet, and had a soft voice and a gentle manner, which suited her tiny presence. Under her hand, these babies came alive. There was David, and Alice, and Peter, and several Joans. Their names were written on tiny white labels at the bottom of their cots. I went in to see the older babies, who owned from four to six months, after I had seen the gardenful.

The house is light, and bright, and pretty. At times, it must hold some of the heaviest hearts in the world, but the eye sees only the patterned cot-covers, the toys, and the flowers. But there I saw a little baby boy, and he saw me.

By this time, the others were gurgling and crowing, and even holding their arms up as if they were trained to it, but the little bald-headed one just looked. He didn't even smile. He was the perfect sportsman. His casting was silent and perfect. His hook is in for good. He was only a few weeks old, and he was tired, and shut his eyes and went to sleep.

I didn't want to make a quick decision. I was in London for a few weeks, anyhow, and wanted to see all the babies there were. I was uneasy. The little one was so bald, and old-looking. I knew that plenty of people would call him ugly. His ears stuck out even more frowardly than jug-handles. He did not smell good, because as the matron said, his food did not seem to agree with him, and he was always being sick. He also seemed to be sore in parts. In fact a baby who didn't feel at home there, and never would.

So I left him. I wandered miserably about London for a couple of days, not doing anything more in the visiting line. Then I said to my husband with a certain amount of guile, 'Would you like to see a few of the babies I've been looking at?'

So at the week-end, we went up to the hostel together. He was astonished at the youth of the children. He had visualized a romping two-year-old, already shouting 'Daddy!' I looked round for what I already called 'my' baby, and didn't see it. I asked what had happened, wondering unhappily if it had already been adopted, but they said it was not well.

'May I see it again?' I asked. (I don't say 'it' about babies, now.)

'Certainly,' said the young and pretty nurse in charge. She led us to a tiny room where 'it' was lying, squinting sarcastically at a pink woollen dog on its pillow. It looked at Kay, my husband, and laughed. And then it began to cough. While it coughed, it rubbed its feet up and down on the sheet, as if to say 'Just wait till I can walk, I'll show this damned cough where it gets off'.

Instead of not being interested in it, Kay liked it very much. 'Isn't it a game little thing?' he asked admiringly. 'If you really want a baby so young, I hope you'll have this one.'

That settled it. We told the creature it was coming to us, and it grinned with the tears from coughing still in its eyes, as if it understood every word we were saying. Then we went downstairs to hear all particulars of its family, why it was there to be adopted, and so on.

And every day for over a week, I went there to learn how to bath and feed what I began to think of as my son. But alas, his cough got worse and worse, and he began whooping away every time he coughed. Though he was isolated in his tiny room, the matron said he would have to be sent away to hospital, as the other children might catch the disease.

So we made a sudden decision after all, and muffled him up and took him away with us. The matron lent us clothes and accessories and even had bottles of food made to last until the following morning. We had two hundred miles to go.

Explorers have discovered new lands, and pioneers have tracked across the desert wastes, and people will keep on going to the North Pole, but now we feel that we have blazed our trail. We eventually got the baby home.

At that time, we lived in a street (for some reason called a drive) in a stone house with two rec. five bed. kit. bath and cellars, as the advertisement had it. And there was a garden, and a fair, fat, faithful maid. But there was nothing at all in it for baby. I had expected to choose one, come home, get everything ready for it, and then go back for the child. But that was not to be.

Fortunately, the time was summer, and warm. We fished out a basket chair, and made a cot of it, with a pillow and a cushion. The baby only weighed eight pounds, so it was easy to carry him about. As soon as I had got him settled for the night at the side of my bed, I went downstairs and scalded his bottles, and washed his one set of clothes, and went about thinking noble thoughts. I also rang up my astonished doctor, to tell him I had got a baby, and asked him if he would call the following morning.

The baby was at the house, so to speak, on approval. Many formalities had to be gone through before he was legally adopted. Two lots of people had to vouch for our respectability, and a guardian *ad litem* was appointed by the city council. This man was very suspicious, and didn't approve of us, or the baby, or the Adoption Society. He asked why we couldn't have got a baby from our own city, and wasn't pleased at all when I said that I was hoping for an intelligent child.

I shall never forget that first night. I didn't sleep, I was too much exalted for that. The baby slept between whoops, as well as he could, and about half-past five began to cry with what I recognized as a hungry sound. I floated downstairs to get food for him. And however much it seems like lying, it is perfectly true to say that I got up every morning for about a year with

22

just the same proud joy to feed this baby. I admit that my enthusiasm had worn a little thinner four years later when I adopted a month-old baby girl, and that I sometimes groaned and yawned 'Oh lord, can it really be six o'clock?' But she was a healthy little wench, and yelled with anger if I was a few minutes late.

Her journey was by train, and took seven hours. I travelled first class. Here, might I say how wonderful are dining-car men in trains? Why does no one sing paeans to them? I will. They brought jugs of water to warm her bottles, they nursed her those odd times I was forced to seek the lavatory, they fed me as though I had done the whole job myself, and quietened passengers who objected to her strenuous yells. All but the head waiter — he was the only married man.

3

It astonishes me to think how very rarely bathwater is just right. It runs usually too hot here, and like oil and water, hot and cold water do not mix. There's sorrow at your feet and pain at your shoulders. This morning, however, it was just right.

That's what makes the story of Goldilocks and the Three Bears so entrancing. The little girl found one of three chairs just right, one of three bowls of porridge just right, one bed out of three just right. True, they were somebody else's, but she got away with that.

What a strange foundation for life fairy tales make. I would not deprive any child of this joy. I don't like much to direct children, either. If they can't see a thing, let them miss it. The little girl found the sea for herself, and said peremptorily to us, 'Stop!' She examined it in an awestruck way for a long time, and then turned to us with her eyes shining and said, 'Water. Boats on it. A lot of water'.

I remember my own first sight of foxgloves at an early age. We were having a picnic somewhere near Bolton Abbey, and the air was very thundery. I had walked away. The air was so still that voices seemed to pierce it, and the sky was a bright greyish green. Then I saw the foxgloves. I have only a faint recollection of the storm that followed, but the foxgloves have never died.

It is good to have a few glowing memories. Life has never been really smooth for me — but can life be smooth for anybody? Just at the moment, there's money, and what goes with it, security. I like living in a nice house, I like comfort, and hot baths, and the good feeling of being physically well and having wide, shallow steps to climb to my bedroom instead of steep and frightening ones. I like my great white bedroom with its mullioned windows facing east and south, and I like not having to wash clothes and crockery, and not being forced to carry out the ashes and bring in the coals. I like to scrub floors and to light fires when I want, but those are simple pleasures now.

All the same, life has never been smooth. I have known the deepest and dreariest of poverty, and when anybody tells me of theirs, my eyes leap instinctively to their shoes. I still think that the most grinding misery of poverty is cardboard shoes — shoes with papery soles, that will not turn even a thin shower of rain. And how sitting about with wet, chilled feet will make even the hardiest throat sore. I used to envy policemen and soldiers and postmen. I used to look in shop-windows and hate the rich and pretend that lovely shoes were silly because they had thin soles.

The thought of comedians in great shoes with large, useless lumps of leather flapping at the front of them would turn my stomach over. I used to look around with eyes of cunning for strong pieces of cardboard, and cut them to size (how often the wrong size!) with blunt scissors, and insert them over the holes or near-holes in my shoes. When the cardboard was new, and I had two pieces, I would gain a new confidence. I would say with satisfaction, 'No sore throat tomorrow'.

And when the comfortable scribes who love wine turn their flippant sneers towards cups of tea, I feel that they need more understanding. I am willing enough myself to see that wine must be a great help and a source of wit to those who need it, because it is a lightener and a lifter, something that runs like sunshine through the dreary landscape of the blood.

Wine costs so much a bottle, ready made. When you have once got over the effort of hospitality (if it is an effort) there is nothing to do but open the bottle and wait. But tea is different, especially tea among the poor. Sometimes it is an effort in itself to go and draw the water for it. Then there's the teapot, and the cups, and the wondering how much or how little you can put in the teapot, the urging of the fire to boil the water; even the washing-up afterwards.

And when the tea is ready, there's the terrible gratitude you feel towards the heat of it pouring down your poverty-cold mouth. It makes your whole frame fill with ambition to fight the beastliness of the world. And it is no false ambition. It gives you a fresh start without leaving a subtle injury behind. Also, you are filled with a more powerful and tenderer gratitude to the ones who make it for you. They know how you are feeling at the moment. Tea, like death, is a great leveller.

But I like champagne with a kind of reverend misery. (Reverend didn't seem to be the right word, but I looked it up in the dictionary, and it is described as (B) awful, so this will do.) On the few occasions when this has been really good, I find that the vintage year is nineteen twenty-eight. And now I am the proud owner of a case of nineteen twenty-eight — but it has a strange, and to me, unknown name on it — Cachet Rouge — which probably serves me right. I know of Bollinger, Moet & Chandon, Veuve Clicquot; but Cachet Rouge is a stranger to me, and may always remain so. The case is in the cellar, the bottles are still wrapped in straw, when perhaps they ought to be out of it, and lying on the cool stone shelves.

There are forty-eight quarter bottles. This, because

a quarter bottle is about my capacity. An eighth bottle would be nearer still, if there were such a thing on sale. I am what is known as a weeping drunk, or would be, if I could get anywhere near drunk. But that delight is not for me. A glass or two, and I begin to think how bloody awful the world really is. I want to do something immediately to set it right, know I can't, and subside, weeping.

I will remember with deepest passion one frond of lacy meadow-sweet against a dark-blue sky, seen through the eyes of a child. I see in every detail an old wooden gate which swung open to a paradise of green and poppied lane dividing a field of ripening corn. The dawn-clouds are once more lying weary on the slopes of Addingham Moorside as the early hush is broken by the ecstatic singing of a dozen larks. And all fond company dies and is gone. And once again, I am alone, still weeping.

The editor who takes me to Rules to lunch always tells me a new funny story, of the kind I have never seen printed. Yet I think they are good enough to print. This is old, now. It was the first one he told me, but I have never forgotten it.

I have no journalistic ability, and could not tell a good story to save my life, but I must put this one down, for I like it, and there may be one or two people who haven't heard it. It's about a clergyman who married, and who, after three months had passed, asked his wife in a very roundabout and stammering way (beautifully imitated by my favourite editor) if she was pregnant. 'No,' said the lady, very kindly and thoughtfully; 'No, I'm sure I'm not.' 'Oh dear, oh dear,' stuttered her husband, wringing his hands, 'and do we have to go through all that *dreadful* business *again?'*

Well, it is very short, shorter than I thought, and my mind seems to be turned away from God this afternoon, and a little away from the truth as well. But these things will happen. I am very much subject to moods, of one sort and another. This has been a poor summer, up north. The trees are heavily in leaf, they sway about in a melancholy manner, as though waiting in a most dreary, windy queue for a performance by the sun, in which the principal actor hasn't turned up.

We did see the sun in May, for we went to the South of France all that month. It was what is called the finish of the season when we arrived, so Mentone was quiet and lovely, and it became our joy to walk in and out of Italy with the children, partly to get our passports well stamped and partly because there is a lovely sandy bay just beyond the point.

The Riviera is renowned for a kind of cardboard prettiness. It looks brittle, yet hard and strong. Rank, rank in its flower masses and colours; red, yellow, purple, blue strike the eye and hurt it. But there are high, greyish hills rising behind the towns, and it was sheer pleasure to ride up the twisting road to the top in the local bus, and wander about on the hilltop; and queer pleasure to find a sprawling signature in the visitors' book in a tiny hotel, Max Baer from Chicago. I looked at it for a long time.

But the Riviera has passed out of my life. There was nothing to keep it there. I may go again if I grow really old, for only the old seem happy there, sitting in the sunshine, in the Workhouse of the Rich.

I have said that I live in an old house, with plenty of

room in it, but I forgot to say that to the other end of it is clamped a farm. As this used to be a very big house before they modernized it in sixteen hundred and twenty-seven, all the barns and cowsheds — laithes and mistals, we call them — are built of the old stone and roofed with stone, too. There are houses like this in the Cotswolds, where wool was the staple industry, as it is in this town.

I did not realize how ugly the north could be until one afternoon, a year or two ago, when I was returning from London. It was a cold, wet, misty and hopeless-looking winter evening, and I saw from the train window that there are far too many hens and hen-houses in Yorkshire, and too much tar and blackness. The philosophy of the hen-owners must be dark indeed, judging from their tarred fences. Oh, for some Prussian blue, or vermilion, or orange, just a small transfer from the opulence of the South of France. But black is the inevitable hue.

It is only winter-ugliness we have here. And winter ugliness can be even fouler in London. This house is never ugly. I don't know whether it is the shape of it, or what. And the stone-roofed barns, which bend in the middle, look very beautiful, whether there's rain, or frost, or sunshine on them. Across the field is the flank of a great colony of Council Houses. I wonder if they will ever blend with the landscape, and mellow, as this house has done.

I am not politically-minded, but I do like the way most of the Council Houses have been built in this town. They lie on the tops of hills, away from the smoke and fumes, in decent-sized gardens. I like them much more than city streets.

I am sure there are some changes in living that are better instead of worse. There is a row of cottages near here. Some of them are mine, now (if anything can really belong to anybody), and I can remember what they looked like thirty-five years ago. I was much more alive as a child than I am today. I have grown used to things. But then, my heart would ache and bleed all the time. I hovered about those cottages, and got my foot into one whenever I could. It seemed to me that misery dwelt in them. One or two were simple and lovely, with their high, polished dressers, wooden chairs and rockers, square tables with clean oilcloth on the top, and bright, gold-rimmed pint pots, and a hanging plant in the window and a cat on the well-kept rag rug.

But the others! A large mangle was the principal item of furniture, because the wife had to take in washing. The husband worked, certainly, but he drank his wages regularly, and if the wife and the many children wanted to eat, she had to wash clothes, day in and day out, and think herself lucky to get the work. There were so many children, there was so much wailing discomfort, and so many drunken quarrels to be smoothed down, that one wondered how the people could find any joy in life. But perhaps they did. Perhaps I only saw and heard the worst of it, without any understanding.

I know things are different today. There's a clean and shining pride down the whole row. Out of those toiling mothers, a new race was born. But what is to come next? Will this just tail off into a kind of slushy, unadventurous softness? I know only too well how soft one gets with a little comfort. My husband and I lived in a tent when we had nowhere else to live, and my stoic heart knows we would go and live in a tent again. But my soft body doesn't want to do that.

4

All of yesterday morning I spent in the Turkish Baths. I have slept the clock round, and it is already twelve o'clock today. This astonishes me. Where have I been this morning? I recollect the dream of walking up hundreds of stone steps to see a marvellous view, but in a state of absolute panic. I do the same thing in real life, with the panic perfectly under control. Now, the degrading progress of this morning is printed on my mind. I have reached the point where imagination and reality meet, and lost not only a morning, but a breakfast as well, which grieves me.

The door of the Turkish Baths opens with a snap, and warm air rushes from behind it. I drifted through the warmth, looked around the well-known place, which was quite empty, found a flat, hard bed and undressed in the cubicle, draped a thin cotton towel around me, and sought the weighing machine, which tremblingly informed me that I was a hundred and thirty-three pounds.

Then I went down some rubber steps, which have a folded towel laid on each one, feeling a little like a Roman, not at all like a Turk. There was life downstairs, because two other women were there, and the two attendants. Since I was here last, the older attendants have retired, and now, these are young girls. One was saying to the other as I entered, 'It's very easy to do the right thing, really, isn't it, Eva?' Eva said Yes, it was.

Could they possibly have meant it? I wondered, as I sat with my feet in a small tin bath half filled with warm water, a rag of wet towelling swathing my head. I trailed into the first hot room, still thinking about 'the right thing'.

There are slabs that look like marble round the sides of these hot rooms. They have pieces of carpet on them, over which is laid a clean towel, and hollowed wooden head-rests, looking like beheading blocks. I like to lie down for an hour, growing gradually warmed and soothed, finding my cares sweating themselves away. Then, after a few minutes in the steam room, I am bathed as if I were a baby — but a very tough baby indeed.

Panfuls of water are thrown over me. I am rubbed with a loofah, and scrubbed with a dog-brush, and then soaped and massaged. I stand under hot and cold showers, am gently dried, then muffled in two great white Turkish towels (is this the reason the baths are called Turkish?), go back upstairs to my waiting bed, have a twopenny cup of tea, sleep for an hour, dress and go home — very often accompanied by a headache, as I stay downstairs too long.

Perhaps women who were badly and cruelly treated in the last life are allowed to be bath attendants in this. They seem to be a contented race. I have known four — simple, good and happy women, shining with that happiness that comes from goodness. One used to ask me to tea in her tiny flat, and I would go there with pleasure. This flat was really one room partitioned off into kitchen, bedroom, and sitting-room. She was an ardent Roman Catholic, and went every morning, wet or fine, to seven o'clock mass.

How much I envied her, she will never know. Oh, to believe in something so much that you will get up every morning at half-past six just to go into a church and pray! And not only to pray, but to be soothed and sanctified for the day. To be able to put on armour every morning is a thing I could not do. I should find holes and thin places in it before an hour was gone.

If I could find God in a church, I should be glad. But I cannot. I go often to sit in churches, both here and abroad, to think about faith and piety, and to be sorry that I possess neither. Now and then I see a good and lovely face, but it is mostly on a very old woman; and it makes me think there might be some consolation in age.

Perhaps I have no deep feelings at all, in the religious sense. I am glad to see young creatures, and leaves, and patterned beetles and snowflakes, and to savour the taste of each season. But life itself is difficult, full of unfinished ends and unfinished thoughts. I once went into Cologne Cathedral just as a service was starting, and saw a beautiful coloured show. The faces around me were moved by some deep feeling; and I stood, alone, frowningly curious but quite cold.

I sometimes wonder which life-scene will break across my dying eyes, if I die slowly enough for that. There are so many that might come, when all bonds grow loose, and scenes that have been locked tightly away break through their doors. The freest of us has a thousand chains.

There are many things I have done in which I glory, and shall never repent, in spite of all the laws of Moses. I have broken several of the commandments with joy. But there is a commandment which I think he forgot to inscribe, and that, I have broken in sorrow. There are times in life when I have done mean things, and those are the most sad of all. I hereby apologize publicly for every mean action I have done in my life.

I am not filled with remorse about any dead people, for the dead can never come back to me, either to reproach, to help, or to praise. No, I cannot recall any one particular mean action, but there must be very many of them, and I wish I could undo them. I make it a point never to break my word to the children.

Nicholas came flying in at lunch-time, his cheeks pink with excitement, scrambled on my knee, gave me a hearty kiss, and said, 'Mother, I'm proud of you!' I don't think either of us had the slightest idea what he meant. What is there to be proud of, in staying in bed until twelve o'clock? He was simply excited, because being free from chicken-pox at last, he had been down to the village to play with his cousins, and had enjoyed himself.

But his speech has done a lot to me. It has made me think that I ought to do some work, and that there *is* great pleasure in being alive. I like everybody much better, and am filled with plans for the future, such as having alterations done near the side door, where everything looks so gloomy in heavy rain.

There is some sunshine today. I am going out into it, with the children. God and the truth might be lurking in some obscure part of the garden. Who knows?

I am glad I had a good mother, though she never practised goodness, nor even thought herself good. Every now and then, she would exert herself, and walk swiftly to the church, a mile away, in which all her eleven children were christened. And she would come back, looking very sheepish, as though she, too, had expected to find God there, and hadn't.

What a strange time she must have had in her seventy-two years. She was married at sixteen to a man ten years her senior, and plunged into uncomplaining maternity over and over again. She was always baking bread and cakes and pies to fill our hungry bellies. How we appreciated her!

We liked company, and had a large table with two wooden leaves to extend it. With six or seven visitors, we often sat down twenty to a meal, and never rose hungry. We were not poor then, it was the war that took away our living.

It seems to me that we lived on bread and fruit, with meat twice a week. We got apples by the barrel, and bananas by the crate. And we always had home-made jam and marmalade, and cheeses from the dales. (And my surgeon told me I was so healthy that it was a pleasure to watch my works go round. He saw them in the course of some fancily named operation when he kindly removed my appendix free of charge.)

One of the nicest days in my life was when I was about four years old, and I suddenly knew what it meant to be alive, to be in a summer garden, with my face to the sun, and at the beginning of something.

I did not know what I was beginning, though I know now, in a sadder way, that I still am. The perfection I was certain of has not happened, and I am going down the falling arc of the circle. There must be perfection somewhere, for I have caught glimpses of it, in curious ways. If I die, and death is annihilation, how shall I know or care? But if I awake, it will be with my face toward the sun again.

My mother was very human, and used to get exasperated with all of us. She would search for words to describe her angry feelings, and has called me a variegated flat fish more than once. When she said she would 'larrup' us, we knew she was only teasing, but if she said she would thrash us, we had to walk our chalks very straight. We were brought up on corporal punishment, and not enough of it, so far as I was concerned. I did things with a kind of delight, knowing I should be punished, and so enjoying them doubly.

I do not remember getting any indelible scars at home — mentally or physically. School did that. And for that reason, I have experimented a little with schools for Nicholas. For a week or two, he has even been away. I thought he ought to know what religious instruction was. So I sent him to a convent.

It seems that there is only one Christ, but that the religion Christianity has got split into a great many sects. I love to read the Bible, and I know that the life of Jesus was a wonderful one, and that all he taught can be condensed into 'Love thy neighbour as thyself' — which is a very hard thing to do. Yet one can give it a sporting chance, or one can try.

Yet what a storm I brought upon my head. Friends of all denominations except Roman Catholic came running to tell me that I was doing a wicked thing. They couldn't explain coherently why, but the burden of their cry was 'They'll get him!' I could not find the correct words to tell them that if my little son found the thing to get a hold of that I had missed, I should be filled with joy and gratitude.

Unfortunately he didn't, and he hasn't. He must have been formed in my way already. The seed fell outside him, not in. He stood calm and cool, six years old, and listened critically. Then he contracted scarlet fever, perhaps in self-defence, and we brought him home in the middle of it, as we had brought him home in the middle of whooping-cough, as a baby.

So off he went to a kindergarten near home, when all that was finished with. And there, after a fortnight, he got chicken-pox. Now it is the summer holidays. At this moment, he is lying on the floor, quietly reading. There are books of every kind in this house, and he is free to choose his own reading matter, as I was. At present, he rather likes *Alice in Wonderland* (which I thought, as a child, was a grown-up book) and Grimm's fairy tales, and, of course, *Everybody's Weekly*.

I have a respectful admiration for Nick. If he can only work his way through school on the illness racket, I will abet him by every means in my power. But there's not much left for him to have, and he has been inoculated against diphtheria, which I have had myself, and which I fear. I am like every other mother, really. I want to grow wings, and spread them over the children, and keep harm away. And I am also sensible enough to know that it is no use. There are no wings to protect one's children.

The sunshine has gone, a cold wind has returned, and darkness has fallen early. Is it an omen? For myself, I do not care. I think I am ready to face anything. I can face evil, for if there is evil, there must also be good. But have I anything to give these little ones?

5

Sometimes, my husband and I go to what is called the 'local' cinema. It stands at the junction of six roads, and though it is no Roxy, it does very well. We pay a shilling, and therefore sit in the best seats in the house, which are in a small gallery, called 'the circle'.

These seats are good and new and comfortable, and each is a kind of armchair, holding two people. We like to sit in the middle of the front row. First of all, we park our car in the spare ground behind the cinema, then we stroll up and visit the sweet shop and get some Gold Flake cigarettes and a few packets of sweets known by my family as 'stingers'. They are two packets for a penny, and if you eat three, you get a sore mouth. They melt fairly rapidly, and sting as they melt, and are probably made of magnesia.

Either the girl in the paybox is beautiful, or I am mistaken. It seems to me that she is very beautiful, and I am struck with fresh wonder each time I see her sitting there doling out the tickets. She knows us, now, and has our shilling tickets ready, and a pleasant smile goes with them. If I had been beautiful, I should have done something about it years ago. I know, and like, several of my own good points — some have been nurtured from the weediest beginnings — but I have never been able to give myself marks for beauty. Like everybody else, I stare earnestly in the mirror at times, and wonder where it is that I fail so completely, but I do not know. I have two eyes, a nose, and a mouth, and a skin without any spots, but the whole effect is just a face. Again, excuse me.

Tonight we went to this cinema. And how we enjoyed it! Like Ouida's hero, I rowed faster than any of them. When I am amused, I laugh aloud, and tonight I have laughed a great deal.

This cinema doesn't show the films one usually sees. These are mostly about small towns in America and whether they are really like the small towns, or not, I do not know. But I like them. I like the father who is henpecked and has to get up early to light the furnace and feed the chickens and let the cat out. I like the pretty daughter who stands by her father and the not-so-pretty daughter who is growing up to be a second edition of her mother.

I know that the father is going to do something spectacular, by mistake, towards the end, and yet, when he does it, no one is more surprised and pleased than I am. In this film, the wife has always held up one Harold Macaulay as a hero, and wished she had married him, and dinned the fact in her husband's ears morning, noon, and night. And he turns out to be the bank robber her husband accidentally exposes, so the tables are pleasantly turned. We know there will be no more Harold Macaulaying by one chastened wife. (Oh, what a horrid man he was, who didn't remember his old flame, and snarled at her and called her 'Fat-face' in front of everybody!) But there was an attempt in this picture to show that there is, after all, plenty of affection even between a henpecked husband and a nagging wife. The audience seemed to like it.

The other film was about an ambitious little school-teacher who wanted her fiancé to leave his small-town reporting and go out into the big world. But when the big world moved for a while into the small town, in the shape of reporters waiting to hear news of an escaping criminal, and something of the life she thought she was wanting came near the little schoolma'am, she anxiously (after the tumult and the shouting had died) asked her fiancé to stay in the small town altogether. Which he obligingly did.

And there was a news film in the middle, about firemen, who now, unhappily, ride to their fires in *buses*, great and somehow obscene-looking buses, instead of those red and gold wagons which they used to ornament so well. Has anybody ever known a body of firemen in private life? Do they look heroic? Surely they must look heroic. They go about doing brave things and dangerous things, and every so often, one will lose his life.

Alas, I do not know a fireman personally! But it is amazing who knows who if you track things to their source. Just think, my father's cousin's wife's sister was nurse to the late T. E. Lawrence. This is the only connection I have with the higher life, and it is a very remote one.

My father used to tell us odd scraps about the way life went on eighty years ago, but it did not seem so very different from the life of today. He is eighty-five now, and is engaged in forgetting all he ever knew.

We could never fill him with our enthusiasms when we were small. He said that his grandfather had trailed him for miles over the countryside when he was a child, every time anything new was heard of, taking him just for company. He had seen every two-headed calf and four-legged chicken within a radius of fifty miles, and all his curiosity had been damped by the gruelling walks he had taken. How we longed for the opportunity to see such wonders! So far as I am concerned, it is still to come. The animals around here seem to be quite normal. Perhaps time has changed all that, now our thoughts have been transferred to human beings born four and five at a time.

The children are playing in the rapidly disintegrating summer house with two shoe-trees and a very rusty lawn-mower. This mower may be done for, but it is not so old. We are born forgetters. We leave things about, in rain, in frost, in snow and in sunshine. But some of them, like Nick's tricycle, win through. Nothing can vanquish them. They are of one spirit with ourselves. The lawn-mower, however, after two years, has given up the struggle entirely. The kindly farmer sent in a young Adonis with a scythe, and for some days, at intervals, we had for company the lovely sound of hand-cut grass falling, and the unforgettable smell of hay drying beneath the windows.

Grass has been so plentiful this year that we have a tremendous hayrick in the stackyard that has been empty except for pigs and old iron since nineteen twenty. It looks beautiful, now, seen through these stone-mullioned windows, but something tells me that the winter sun will hide coyly behind it, and visit us no more. And if I know my half-cousin, the farmer, as well as I think I do, the rick will stand there until it rots.

And still the mornings come in cold and grey, and the heavy leaves move gently in a light but chilly breeze. Many of them do not know they are moving for the last time. This afternoon, some of the larger branches are to be sawn off, for the house is becoming tree-buried, and the sky has been seen only through a network of leaves since spring.

I was up early today, re-reading P. D. Ouspensky's *New Model of the Universe*. I grieve to say I have marked my copy, and written in the margins, a thing which I have never done to a book before. Something must have stirred me deeply the first time I read it.

Chapter two is called *The Fourth Dimension*. Now

when I stand before (or even in) that, I realize that here is something I know nothing about.

> The greater part of our being lives in the fourth dimension, but we are unconscious of this greater part of ourselves. Or it would be still more true to say that we live in a fourth-dimensional world, but are conscious of ourselves only in a three-dimensional world. This means that we live in one kind of conditions, but imagine ourselves to be in another.

We can live in several kinds of confusions, too, and I am like the child in the fairy tale, and will still cry out that the king has no clothes on.

> At the very beginning, when defining the idea of the fourth dimension, I pointed out that if it existed, it would mean that besides the three perpendiculars known to us there must exist a fourth. And this in its turn would mean that from any point of our space a line can be traced in a direction unknown and unknowable for us, and further that quite close, side by side with us, but in an unknown direction, there lies some other space which we are unable to see and into which we cannot pass.

Doesn't this mean, simply, that we know very little actually, but there's no limit to our imaginations?

It is strange to know that Mr Ouspensky has crammed the research of twenty-one years into forty-five pages, all very much like the above quotations. He tells you what the Fourth Dimension is. He says it is the Fourth Dimension. In forty-five pages. He is a clever man, but no nearer heaven than I am.

If I were a fetish worshipper, the object of my worship would be trousers. But probably it is the men within

42

the trousers that I like. Yet I stare at trousers with the warmest curiosity. They are all so different. I know my friends by their trousers. Hang up the trousers, and I think I could say 'There's Tom, or Dick, or Harry'.

Unfortunately, the dictionary definition of fetish is: 'an object, either natural or artificial, capable of being appropriated by an individual whose possession of it procures the services of a spirit lodged within it.' I cannot help liking Ecclesiastes, whether or no he wore trousers, who said:

> I will be wise; but it was far from me.
> That which is far off, and exceeding deep, who can find it out?
> I applied mine heart to know, and to search, and to seek out wisdom, and the reason of things, and to know the wickedness of folly, even of foolishness and madness: And I find more bitter than death the woman, whose heart is snares and nets, and her hands as bands: whoso pleaseth God shall escape from her: but the sinner shall be taken by her.
> Behold, this have I found, saith the preacher, counting one by one, to find out the account:
> Which yet my soul seeketh, but I find not: one man among a thousand have I found: but a woman among all those have I not found.

6

I have spent four hours in hospitals this week. Three of them flew, for I was accompanying my sister, whose neck has become too much like that of a Burne-Jones model. She has shown no symptom of any other disease, therefore she is an interesting case, and everybody who saw her seemed pleased and alert, with an 'Ah, here is something different!' air.

We walked into a large, concrete-floored room, which reminded me of much I have read about modern Russia. (This is a very modern hospital.) We were told to be there at eleven, and were fifteen minutes early, but all the seats were taken by waiting people. There would be perhaps a hundred of them, and another hundred arrived later. The room was big enough to hold us all without any crowding.

Everything proceeded in an orderly way. The first people queued up at a desk, passed up their doctors' letters, and obtained 'books', and then went and sat in the waiting-rooms assigned to the various surgeons. With some pomp and ceremony, the surgeons and their assistants arrived.

I know that surgeons are noble men, and that they give their services to hospitals free, but the sight of them always makes me laugh. I laugh inwardly, but none the less thoroughly, because I know a lot of their tricks. They look as clean-cut, but not always as hand-some, as men in advertisements; their dark-rimmed glasses ooze self-confidence to the sheep-like mob around them, their white overalls shine like iced cakes. They smile a smile at the corner of the ceiling which momentarily embraces humanity; but more by way of a celestial minuet than a waltz. Doors close behind them with a sharp click.

All patients in this new and shining hospital have to watch two doors, for a lighted sign saying 'Next Patient' appears on them at intervals. And the waiting people look like spectators at a tennis match, their heads turning quickly one way, then the other. For there is nothing much to see but these doors and each other.

After we had sat there for two hours, we saw that there was a large, clean buffet, where tea was being sold at a penny a cup. We were by that time naturally tired, and the first excitement had worn off, so we went for two cups. The girl behind the counter made some fresh tea in a large enamel teapot of a bright red colour. It was good tea.

The assistant fell to us. I went into his room, because I saw no reason for remaining outside. This man was a cheerful, clean young Scot, who smiled pleasantly, and actually led us to two chairs, saying it was as cheap to sit as to stand. He asked my sister many questions, and wrote the answers gravely down, as if he were at the trial scene in *Alice in Wonderland*. Then he stared for a while at his writing, and went for the other doctor, after telling my sister to go into an inner room, 'and take off some of y'r things'.

They came back soon, accompanied by an impassive-looking nurse, and went through all the questions again, with actions this time, listening and tapping and so on. They discovered the scar of an old operation, and asked excitedly who had done it, and when. And still, there were no symptoms.

Then the older doctor attacked. 'Something should be done about this,' he said. 'Are you willing to come in now?'

My sister wasn't. She only wanted to be an outpatient. The two men were not at all disturbed. The time was then half-past one, and they still had hours of work in front of them, but they talked the whole thing over thoroughly, and decided to give X-ray a sporting chance. They telephoned to the X-ray department, and we finally went there so that the people in charge could have a look at this swan-like neck. They cheerfully said they would treat it every Saturday morning at half-past nine, so I presume they will.

People can be charming, but I feel that charm is wasted in a hospital. All the time, I felt as if somebody was standing on my back, pressing my head into cotton wool. There was nothing whatever the matter with me, yet when I saw a telephone booth, I groped my way towards it, rang up home and said to my husband, 'Will you come for us? We will be standing at the gate'. He said he would, and we waited in the drizzle, under a tree, looking at the new, yellow drive bordered with flowers.

Yesterday, I saw one of those things which was just a little different. I went to visit my father in hospital. He is in a much older hospital, a place with green-distempered walls, varied by coy black flutings which radiate from behind hot water pipes. And there are orderlies in clean white suits instead of female nurses in clean white aprons, because this is a ward full of old men, and old men have sometimes to be looked after like babies, though these men are very different indeed from babies.

In two years at home, my father has worn out three nurses, and brought many grey hairs to the heads of young people. So when his doctor at last suggested that he should be removed to hospital, there was no dissentient voice. He is eighty-five, almost blind, almost deaf, and when he is not sleeping, has a kind of querulous obstinacy which shakes him like a wind. His illness is accompanied by a strange smell. He is not in pain, though the daily dressings must be uncomfortable for him.

When we arrived at the hospital, he was fast asleep. We tiptoed delicately to the centre of the ward, and got two wooden chairs to sit on, bringing them to the side of the bed. If you make up your mind resolutely to ignore the smell, you get used to it. We sat for a while, looking at all the other old men and their visitors. Then I surveyed my father with the same bland indifference with which I have looked at him all my life.

I know that he is my father, and that in many ways mentally I am like him. But he has always been a complete stranger to me. I have no affection for him, and it astonishes me that he has any for me. He has, a little; but only, I think, because he can distinguish me from his other ten children by some peculiarity. He never becomes confused about me, though when I mention the children, he frowns, because he knows that I have no children.

I studied his face on the pillow. He has a white beard and thin white hair, and now, a parchment coloured face, because he has been in bed since winter. But there is no softening in that countenance, even in the face of approaching death. He sleeps in a truculent manner, beard in air. He was little, and thin. He is now very little and very thin; a bag of bones held tightly in skin. He will hang on, just to life's fringe, with all the power that is left in him. He does not want to die, ever.

After a moment or two, my sister woke him. She did not want him to miss a minute of our precious company. He opened his eyes, kissed us with his beard, and said eagerly, 'Have you brought my fugit?'

Every week or so, I buy him a tin of Aunt Barbara's Creamy Fudge. He has got the idea of *tempus fugit* and fudge completely mixed in his head, and fugit always comes out instead of fudge. He could hardly hide his impatience until I opened the tin and gave him a piece. Then he went on eating it as fast as he could, opening his mouth like a young bird, and saying 'More!' and being angry if more was not immediately put on his tongue.

He suddenly asked how my husband's mother was going on. She has been dead for nearly four years. So I answered 'Quite all right'. But now and then he will remember things. About my brother, he said sarcastically, 'Ralph's going a long way for his holiday, isn't he?' Ralph had visited him the preceding Wednesday, to take him tobacco and matches, and had said that he was going to the Shetland Isles with his thirteen-year-old son. We do think of places like that in our family — somewhere far away in a corner, unfrequented, and so marvellously worth seeing that we come back dumb, as I did once from Cape Wrath. But the wandering part of us has come from my mother, who would walk until she could walk no more, where it was quiet and there were hills.

My father was the sort of man who occasionally took us to a theatre for a birthday treat when we were young, and made us come out before the end.

We had taken a ham sandwich and some Eccles cakes for his tea, and when the orderlies came round with stacks of bread and butter, my sister said to him, 'Shall you want any bread and butter, or have you enough here?' He answered, 'I want some bread'. But the man passed him by, knowing that he had as much as he could eat. Even when his tray was laid, and a bib tied round his neck, he insisted on eating another piece of fudge. Then he plunged into his meal, eating quickly and ferociously, like a caterpillar, and was tired long before the end, so that we had to put some of it away in his locker.

Sometimes people walked away from a bed, and then more came in. Each ticket of admission was for two people only. There was one old man without a visitor, and he slept all the time. I kept looking round the ward at these super-clean old men, nearly all of them looking angry, irritable, and dissatisfied. I could not see any love in their faces.

Then a young man without a hat came walking in, carrying a little tin box. I followed his progress. He walked up to each old man, spoke a word or two, and gave him a small present, either a twist of tobacco or a packet of sweets.

My sister said, 'Isn't that man *good*? He comes in every week and does this'. I thought about him as he went the round of the ward, patting the old men on their unresisting faces, and saying his odd word or two. He came to my father, smiled, probably for our benefit, as my father could not see him, and said, 'Well, dad, you're looking champion today', and handed him some toffees in a white paper bag. Then he went across the ward and began to cut up some thick twist tobacco for an old man who couldn't do it for himself.

I went over to the man, and said, 'My sister tells me you come and do this every week. Do you?'

He said 'Yes', so I asked him if he would let me help a little, and I gave him a ten-shilling note. He said he would only accept it for The Cause. I said 'Of course it's for the cause', in some perplexity, not seeing what else it could be for. He thanked me, and asked if I wanted a receipt. I said 'No', and began to walk away. But I was filled with curiosity still, so I went back, and said — not rudely, but in quest of knowledge —

'Whatever makes you do this?'

'God,' he said, looking at me very solemnly.

My heart leapt. I hadn't been thinking of my search, and here was, perhaps, something. The young man was saying, 'Haven't you found him?'

'No,' I said, backing, for it is the invariable custom of very earnest people to come close to one's face when speaking, 'But I never stop looking'.

'What made you do this?' he asked, opening the hand into which I had put the note.

'So that the old men could have some sweets at my expense,' I said.

'Oh, no,' he said, coming closer and being more earnest than before, 'It's God being made manifest in you'.

I made a polite and smiling protest as I backed still farther.

'Are you coming every week?' he asked, and I told him 'No', but that I should probably see him again some time.

'I should very much like to talk to you,' he said.

But it is most likely that I shall not meet the young man again. We could never see eye to eye. His simple faith is not simple faith, but most complicated, it seems to me. There is no peace in it. I felt quite uneasy until he had shut up his box, come across to my father, given him two extra pats on the face as a kind of spiritual discount, said 'Aye', in a low, slow voice with his head on one side, and gone away.

Ten years ago, my father could and did quote Shakespeare appropriately on occasion. He was interested in literature and philosophy. But all he said when the bell rang, and we got up to go, was, 'Put that fugit where I can get at it'.

7

Bank Holiday Monday! This is a perfect day, warm and sunny, with a slight, cool breeze. Yesterday was so hot that at night we all slept like the dead, and I have lived through another long and troubled life in a dream.

On Saturday, I sent the two maids away for a fortnight's holiday, my sister came to stay, and we are running the house between us in a haphazard but pleasant sort of way. I get up first to light the fire that heats the water, dress the children, and cook breakfast.

I do not know by what miracle it has come about, but baby, who is put to bed at six every evening, flushed and sleepy, never wakes until eight the following morning. She refuses a midday nap with scorn, now she is over two; and though I am raising her contrary to regulations, she certainly looks well on it. Nick tries to sleep until nine, but this is all part of his desire to sleep schooltime away, and he has not yet realized that the holidays are upon him.

Young children in the early morning are extraordinarily charming. Mine always have an evening bath, so they are still fresh and sweet. During the day, they become more and more grubby. I make faint efforts, at times, to rouse in them a desire for cleanliness, but it is, on the whole, unsuccessful. Perhaps that is why I like to look at them before and during breakfast. When she plays in the garden, baby has a habit of digging with a spade, and throwing the dirt over her shoulder, but not far enough.

There was a day when Nick and his cousin Donald

found a can of liquid tar in the stackyard, and painted each other from head to foot. We heard their delighted yells of laughter, and very soon they came running to show us the result. It was really arresting. Their eyes shone like jewels out of Ethiopian darkness.

They took their cleaning up in a most philosophic spirit. I wanted to put them in the bath as they were, but arriving visitors shrieked that that would 'set' the tar more firmly. So we found olive oil, and rubbed them to the foundations with it. The clothes they were wearing were done for. They remember that as a very satisfactory day, but have never tried to repeat it.

Over and over again, I tell myself that it is impossible to live another person's life. I think a thousand horrors each time Nick is ten minutes late from school; yet he wants to come home alone, so I let him come home alone. And he has nearly a mile to walk. But so, I remember, had I. And I liked the walk — most of all when it rained, and I could make dams in the gutters — but it was a lonelier road then. It is the same when there is silence in the garden for more than ten minutes. For I do fear the sudden, sad evil of people. The children together are all right — they must settle their own differences without my interference. Squalls and yells are part of their education.

And this is where I am quite certain there is no God of the kind I was told about when I was young, no God who sees the sparrow fall. Because he could not see a helpless sparrow fall without having his celestial heart broken.

The fewer people there are in a house, the less work there is to do. Now there are only five of us, and only four beds to make. My husband and I keep to the old-fashioned idea of sleeping together, because we

52

like each other. We have a feather bed, and stick to it winter and summer. I was born in one. I read in some book the other day that it is an almost impossible task to conduct a confinement in a feather bed. What a good thing my mother's doctor did not know that, or where would the eleven of us have been?

Yes, the maids went home on Saturday, and it is now Monday, and there does not seem to be a great deal left to eat — the remains of a joint of beef, some tomatoes, potatoes, and onions. And groceries, and last year's jam, and honey and fruit, and plenty of home-baked bread.

Whatever made me say 'there does not seem to be a great deal left to eat?' Perhaps because I have been used to more for a little while. The luck that is with us now may not last beyond this moment, but it is strange and good to know that at present our whole existence is not just a struggle to get something to eat. There is a breathing space for us, a time to sit down and look around, a time to listen.

And though the world may be sinking to ruin around, I cannot help it. I am drunk with being glad to be alive! The real miracle of summer sunshine, the trees waving their leaves in the immemorial way though kingdoms fall, the grass having the same smell as ever, the sight of new fire leaping through wood and coal, the direct glance from the children's eyes — all this mixes before me and makes a peculiar joy. I know that there is suffering all around me. But cannot I be free?

No, alas, I cannot. I hate the evil and the injustice. If there could be a crusade against that, would I not take a banner in my hand, tell the children to grab my skirts from behind, and set off to the wars? I would. But something yet makes me wake each morning and laugh, and I will not deny that laughter. When I laugh,

I seem to see and hear more clearly than ever before, and to be sure that life is the greatest good we can ever know. It is the miracle, the burning fire — perhaps the god itself.

It is still Bank Holiday Monday. After lunch, my sister decided that we should collect my sister-in-law and her two children, and visit a brother who has hurt his foot by stepping on a plank with a rusty nail in it. I did not want to go, but she said the exercise would do me good, and in a few minutes, though I opposed the project strenuously, she was acting as though I had given my consent, and even washing and changing the children.

That is the way we behave in our family if we really want anything. We act as though we are going to get it, and we do get it, and thus somebody is satisfied every few days.

The wife of the brother we were going to visit spends nearly all her time knitting. She can do remarkable things with a ball of wool and two needles. If a manufacturer of wool decides to advertise a new kind or colour by sending the present of a jumper to some dear little film star, it is Ella who sits down and knits it. I like to see her now and then. I admire her uncanny cleverness. But still I tried to get out of going. It was too hot. I wanted to sit and do nothing whatever. I said, 'It's Bank Holiday. They'll have gone out, surely?'

My sister thought for a minute, and answered, 'How can they go out if Ralph's foot is hurt?'

I gave in, and put baby in a light go-cart, and set off to collect the others. Nick walked by my side, looking very smart in scarlet flannels and a white blouse, wearing a huge sunhat which we had brought from Spain years ago, and is always referred to by us as the Spanish sunhat to distinguish it from the more shrinking kind

54

we brought from the south of France.

My brother Ralph lives two miles away, at the bottom of a steep hill. My heart sank as I thought of pushing a pram four miles on a hot afternoon. But all went well until the two children we had collected on the way began to cough very strongly and peculiarly. This is the first day of freedom from our own chicken-pox quarantine — for baby had it after Nick. Is she now to go straight on to whooping cough? Life has been hard enough for the children this last year or so. I like our local doctor, but not exactly as an attachment to the estate. Must I keep an ear open for whoops?

The hill was longer than I thought, the afternoon hotter. But the family was in, and we were soon drinking tea. Nick accidentally knocked my cup over, on to a pretty tea-cloth, and from that to the carpet, and never even said he was sorry. But I was sorry in more ways than one, for I forgot to ask for more tea, and rose to face that hill unrefreshed.

It was hard, and I am not used to pushing babies up steep hills. When we had gone a little way, the child wanted to get out, and instead of making vague promises to her, I let her climb out. She insisted on pushing the go-cart. The whole thing looked very reasonable to me. I thought she would soon tire.

She pushed that thing steadily up the hill, with frequent turns for a run down, and as her disposition is mischievous and happy — an irresistible combination — I had to let her do as she wanted, and she took a long time over it. When a hand was put out to help her, she indignantly struck it off. Instead of walking two miles back, I am sure I walked four. In the end, because my patience was finished, I thrust her into the folding chair.

And then she yelled — yelled as if she were being tortured. Sweat poured down my back. Nick came up, and said very loudly, 'Don't ill-treat that baby!' He then put his arms around her neck and crawled along while she wept in his ear. This made my progress slower still.

The sun had stopped shining, and Nick had given me his huge hat to hold. The pram wheel had run over baby's sun-bonnet, and it was covered with oil, and I had to hold that, too. I had been so slow in coming up the hill that the others were far in front of me. They waited at the top, and laughed, but my sense of fun had deserted me.

It was so late when we got back to where the whooping children lived that their father, another brother of mine, had prepared a meal, with salad, and beaten raspberries and cream. We put all the children in the raspberry canes (they had eaten at the other house) and went inside, and I fell on a loaf, cut three half-inch slices, covered them with blackcurrant jam, and ate until I was satisfied.

It was reminiscence evening for the Northern wireless programme, and as we ate, we kept singing pre-war tunes — 'You were coming through the corn, Molly Dear', and 'I wouldn't leave my little wooden hut for you', and 'The Old Rustic Bridge by the Mill'. My brother got two plates out of the cupboard and danced, clapping his plates like tambourines. It was the eighth anniversary of his wedding, and he was very happy.

Now it is dark. People keep on dying, and being born. The evening is so very warm that for the first and only time this year, we are without fires. It is quiet. When I went up to Nick's room, half an hour after he had been put to bed, I found him sprawled fantastically on his stomach, with his solitary pillow perched on the bedhead. It seemed to me that he had been working out some grievance on that pillow.

I made the bed comfortable, and turned him on his side. He opened his eyes, and said 'I promised you I would go straight to sleep, and I have gone straight to sleep.' And so he had, he was off before I had tiptoed out of the room.

Yes, the evening has mellowed, and we have all mellowed. My sister is pleased to find that my brother's foot is not so bad as she had feared. And I am sure that I shall not take that particular walk again for a long time. What is the use of walking along hard pavements simply for the sake of spilling tea on somebody's tablecloth? I never once thought of my search for God, and the children would have been much better off playing in the garden.

A friend of ours called. He owns a few shops in rather a squalid quarter of the town, and he has to go round every Saturday to collect his rents. He had let one shop to a barber, and the other day, when this man was in it alone, a woman came in and asked if he would trim her hair for threepence. He had nothing to do at the time, and so said he would. His customer began to make very immoral overtures to him, saying that all could go in for the same threepence. He was terribly afraid, but went on cutting her hair (he is a little man, yet valiant in the safeguarding of his honour) and said, 'Haven't you got a husband, missus?'

'I have,' said the woman, 'but he's doing time, and somebody's got to do something about it.'

Luckily, a man came into the shop, and the little barber got rid of his not-so-fair customer. And when our friend called for his rent, he found his tenant painting some words in Indian ink on a piece of white cardboard to hang outside. He had also written the same words with soap in large, shaky handwriting on all his mirrors, NO LADIES HAIR CUT HERE.

And now, Bank Holiday ends. The darkness is intense, and we may have thunder tomorrow. Of course, there must be a storm after this day.

If God does sit in the sky listening, what strange prayers will rise to him tonight out of this hot, strange darkness. So many people will have been cut down like storm-seared barley since this morning dawned; so many thoughtless acts will have led and will still lead to tragedy; so many small kindnesses will have helped to raise new faith in humanity.

But we are all moving different ways, and there is no look of order in the thing. Consequences have become deranged. If you step in front of a swiftly-moving vehicle you may escape, without damage, you may be hurt slightly or badly, you may be killed. It seems to be a matter of luck.

But so far as I am concerned, here I am, freshly bathed and ready to go to a clean and comfortable bed, grown softer than ever, so that a few miles of walking makes me sick with tiredness. To what end is this waste of time, and thought, and effort? What *is* the use of life? It grows more and more amazing to me that I love it so well.

8

I keep walking out into the warm garden, and back under the green-striped sunblind — used principally to keep out the bluebottles — into the cool house to remind myself of the fact that it is really summer. The trees have been thinned, several large branches were sawn off, and though the millions of small, yellowish flies which lived under the leaves are now homeless, the sun shines again on our mossed green walls.

Is it possible that it is a month since I was in London? I go up every few weeks, and now it is a month since I was there. It seems longer, because the last time I went, I immediately left it again.

I share a flat with a friend. When I got there, after climbing the sixty-six steps, I found she was out, and my telegram of warning was lying on the hall floor. The hall is the size of two hearthrugs, but through its window, the whole stunning frontage of the British Museum is to be seen. From my bedroom, one corner of it looks exactly like a station. I can sit up in bed and think I have arrived.

I went steadily through her list of friends, and then telephoned the place where I thought she would be. I was right. She was in a charming Georgian house in Blackheath, which teems with educated poets, and Siamese cats, and German cooks, and pictures with candles in them, and delicious small girls aged three, in bloomers of blue linen, with wreaths of ivy twining their naked torsoes, and baby boys for ever sunning themselves in sunny gardens.

Vast quantities of work pile up in this house, so that

it seems to me like a clean, refined, and tabulated Caledonian market. It is filled with statistics instead of junk. But they come from all corners of the country in envelopes instead of lorries and handcarts, and have to be sorted out and made use of or destroyed. Books are made out of them, as homes are formed from what is in the Caledonian market, so that here, as there, is an appearance of life busily and usefully lived.

Whenever there is any childish illness — chicken-pox was then fading in Nick, and threatening in baby — I keep away from other children, in case I could bring harm to them. I never know the difference between infectious and contagious diseases — one cannot remember everything. So I did not go up to Blackheath.

It rained, and London seemed uniformly grey. I had a sudden longing for new places. So when my friend arrived, we went almost immediately to Paddington station. I had never been to Paddington, but took her word for it that it was a good station.

When we got there, two rather fine-looking trains were waiting. One was going south-west, and the other north-west. We asked the ticket-collector if he knew of any good towns or villages to visit, and he was a little mystified. 'Where do you want to go?' he kept asking.

Of course we could not tell him, as we didn't know ourselves. My friend had packed a small weekend case, as she thought the weather might be fine, and she wanted to enjoy herself in a lighter frock and shoes, but I had only a nightdress in a brown-paper bag with a bunch of bananas printed on it. I like to travel light, though I have never before travelled as light as this, and when the trip was halfway through, I was compelled to buy a kind of shopping bag with wooden handles, because I had begun to accumulate things, and I got tired of carrying bunched parcels from bus to bus.

The north-west collector came up, and the south-west one told him our difficulty. He was most enthusiastic. 'Can you go anywhere you want?' he asked hopefully.

'Well, not anywhere,' we answered, 'but have you any really nice places — we don't mind how quiet they are.'

Each collector praised his own train. We looked at them. They were very nice trains, there was nothing to choose between them. We were distracted. Should we get on with platform tickets, and just drop off when we came to a good station?

'Have you anywhere between fifteen shillings and a pound?' we then asked. 'That's about the distance we want to go.'

Northwest crowed. He had Tetbury. Southwest was all for Torquay, though it was farther and dearer. We jeered at Torquay, and that settled it. Tetbury sounded right. We went and got our tickets, and a carriage to ourselves.

As soon as the train had set off, the guard came in. He was a countryman with a fine west-country accent. Not only that, but he knew Tetbury.

'What's it like?' we asked.

'Very quiet. Very aristocratic,' he said. 'Plenty of trees. It's hunting country.'

We looked at each other a little wildly, with visions of inhospitable lodge-keepers' houses. I had a wish to sleep in a country cottage, a long way from the road.

He told us all he knew of Tetbury, but forgot to mention that we had to change trains at Kemble Junction, and if we hadn't seen a notice on the platform, we should have landed miles away from our objective.

A tiny train was waiting on the other side of the platform, and it made a very leisurely track between small stations until it reached its goal — the end of the line. This was Tetbury.

We walked up a steep hill into the town, and examined it thoroughly. It is fascinatingly beautiful. We grew more and more tired, but could not stop staring. The evening was full of light, and Tetbury looked in that light more like an Italian town every moment. We could not believe that we were within a few hours' train-ride of London.

Night fell, and we slept in beds made of policemen's helmets, in an old, mysterious house. The landlady seemed to be on the point of holding a jumble sale in any one of the many rooms. Either she was just moving into the place or just moving out. Surely nobody could live in the state of confusion as there was there, with rolled up carpets and sewing machines and bundle after bundle of old clothes tied negligently with string. I put a great spray of paper flowers into the mouth of a yellow china elephant — one of a family of ten which ornamented the piano top — the next morning. It seemed appropriate, for in the room where we had breakfast, there was a black hat hanging on a pair of bellows, and three different people came in to look for Aunt Annie's bag.

The next day we spent riding about in buses. Our spirits lightened as soon as we left that house of mystery. We had lunch at the George in Nailsworth, to which we came by very roundabout stages, and one tea at Stroud and another one at Dursley. After the second tea, we leapt on a bus that was going to Wotton-under-Edge. But we never got to Wotton-under-Edge, for we suddenly leapt off that bus. We saw a village with a strange sight in it — that of people all dressed in their Sunday best, and all going one way.

We asked what was the matter, when we had composed ourselves, and were told 'It's the feet'.

It is a good thing to arrive in a village when the yearly fête is being held, because life is at its best then. The people who do go are determined to enjoy themselves, and the people who don't are dreamy and at the same time tolerant. There is a feeling of 'now' in the air.

We went to one of the two inns, and asked if we could stay the night. At first, the landlady thought not. She had her sister-in-law with her, and her reply was a kind of self-defence. We immediately laughed, because of the funny way we had behaved in unison, stopping the bus, and being sure we were going to sleep in this particular three-gabled pub. We liked the look of the landlady, too, and when she saw us laughing at ourselves, she took us up to a room with two beds in it, and asked if it would do. It looked very good to us.

We went down to a meal of bread and cheese and bitter, with a great bowl of salad as a woman's throw-in. But there were no spring onions. I would not have said anything, but my friend is very firm, especially about spring onions.

I said, 'Oh lord, you know what women are — always wanting something — glasses of water and clean plates and just another fork and the bread cut thinner, please. Can't you be satisfied with things as they are?'

I was wrong, then, as often. She asked for onions, and got them right away. 'We had them ready', the landlady said, 'but we thought maybe you wouldn't like them.'

She was a lovely landlady, one of the nice women of the world, and the next morning, which was Sunday, she lent us two prayer-books, of the reign of King Edward the Seventh, and a large brown umbrella, and saw us off to church, in the softly falling rain. It was the first time I had been to church for seventeen years.

We were to come back to lunch. She cooked us a chicken, and two lots of greens, and a pudding.

We were rather tired after church, in which the vicar (who, before the service, walked up the aisle trailing his surplice after him on some errand of his own, regardless of the congregation) told us in his sermon, that David's was 'a god after man's heart'. *His* heart did not seem to be in his job after 'the feet', which was apparently a church feet, for within ten minutes of beginning to read from his notes, he dismissed us abruptly.

The village was altogether so charming that we decided to leave it immediately after tea so that our dream would never break. But that village is there waiting, and now we know it is there. It has its share of imperfections, of course. The water has to be drawn from a pump on the green, and modern sanitation is unknown. It is on the road to nowhere in particular, and from nowhere in particular. Motorists pass it.

High on the hill above it, overlooking the estuary of the Severn and the mountains of South Wales, stands a grim-looking monument, commemorating Tyndale, the man who did something to the Bible, which I have ungratefully forgotten.

The garage man keeps the great nine-inch key to this stone column, and for threepence, he will let you have the loan of it. On the Saturday night, before supper, we walked to this place, and went up the darkly turning stone steps, and saw the hills and valleys, and the perfect evening sky, and after supper, having found the name Waterley Bottom on the map, took a stroll there, looking for the site of a Roman villa. We didn't find that, but we found a kind of peace which it is very hard to come across on stone pavements.

Perhaps there are people with calm and peaceful souls who are the same in town or country. Though saintly faces look better on the dead than on the living. How can a man look around him with seeing eyes for more than ten minutes and dare to let his soul rest in peace?

I suppose the way to be a good cook is to care immensely for what you are doing. We had a simple and easy meal today, but every part of it was perfect. When my sister boils new potatoes, she puts a sprig of mint in with them, and boils them slowly, so that they have a real flavour of their own. I made parsley sauce for the grilled plaice, and a chef could not have dished up better. At eight o'clock in the morning, I had put a rice pudding in the oven, but what a pudding that turned out to be! There was nothing in it but a handful of rice, three tablespoonfuls of sugar, a lot of milk and a little salt; and five hours' slow cooking. This was really a children's meal. But not a scrap of it was left beyond the fish-skin.

There is one part of me which greatly wants to be a good cook, but I suppress it. It is a kind of road to ruin. If I went along that road, I should look for God and the truth no more. My mind would be intent on flavours and sauces. I should have a garden full of herbs, and a quantity of fat friends. No, I'll do it when I have to, but I will not make cooking my reason for being on earth.

The body is an awful temptation from one end to the other. I like to keep within bounds, and not be an offence to onlookers. But I am already on the slide. Dresses which I had made this year no longer fit me. I cannot close my eyes to the fact. Outsize is yet a name to me, but I tax 'woman's' to the utmost.

A voice whispers in my ear, 'Let go, let go. And then you'll have no other problems. Let life become one long, greasy chuckle. The fatter you are, the happier you'll be.' It is a voice I don't like.

This day finishes without thunder, in an intense and heavy heat. There is no stir, even of air, in the dark silence. The earth seems to be standing still, but we know that cannot be so, because we were told that the earth goes round without ceasing. Night follows day, and day follows night. We were told that, too. Yet how many times, especially in a state of unaccustomed fatigue, do we feel on the point of opening a door that leads to the unknown. We are on the verge of some new country of the mind — but we are dragged back, cruelly.

I cannot leave my body and travel the ether with my spirit, except in dreams. My dreams have no communication with this body as I know it. But I look forward to death as one looks forward to a new kind of holiday. Yet what have I done to deserve this holiday?

I am in outer darkness, and it seems light to me. No voice has called 'Samuel, Samuel', nor have I ever been able to reply, 'Speak, for thy servant heareth'. And yet, after this life of nothing done, death will come to me. When I was young, I thought there was something wonderful to do. There was money to get, but that didn't trouble me. I felt it would come, but it has a habit of turning to leaves in the hand. In any case, I don't like to have money, but only to spend it. For two years, we have had to pay the government surtax, so there must be some, but I am certainly not what is known as a good manager. Our house is a pleasant place, and I can do more or less as I like. But there are so many things to do that I am always as hard up as if I hadn't got a cent.

This heavy silence grows deeper and deeper, the

moments are prolonging themselves into eternity. My mind seems to be wedge-shaped, and the corner of it is prising away a corner of the world.

Baffled! And that by a bluebottle, which flies frenziedly around the room, peering into the lights of the two lamps. I have chased it with a newspaper, as Death at this minute may be chasing me. Each time the insect sees the brilliance of the light, it may think it has a mystic revelation. How am I to know? Why should I dislike this bluebottle fly? I am afraid of his noise, and the aimless look of him. What does he want? Is God afraid of us, with our senseless singing and shouting and dancing?

The holy silence falls again, and I remember that it is Tuesday, and that I have an affection for Tuesdays. There is a Tuesday that I remember with the liveliest gratitude, when a favour was done to me that I cannot forget.

And once, when I was a very little child, a boy I knew and terribly admired flung a packet of sweets for me over the school wall. He was dressed in white flannels — he had on long trousers for the first time — and his beauty overwhelmed me. I could not see why I had been singled out for this wonderful gift. This happened over thirty years ago, but now, if I meet him, I blush and pale alternately, and cannot say half a dozen words to him, because I suffer from disproportionate gratitude.

It needs much more than a careless gesture to waken my grateful feelings now, and the sensation is not so prolonged. It is already Wednesday, for midnight has come and gone, and I have been thinking with too much delight of an almost perfect generosity which has long taken me farther than the farthest star.

9

The storm broke somewhere, though not here. It is now cool and dull again. Can it really be that summer is over, and that the old joke of three days and a thunderstorm is true?

My sister went out for the morning, to visit the hospital for her X-ray, and to do some shopping, and as I went about the household chores, I began thinking about marriage.

My husband and I were married in the last year of what is known as the Great War, so that I was never a young bride, flitting about a newly furnished house, cooking experimental meals for a husband who came home every evening. Our assets were twenty-five pounds and a New Imperial J.A.P. motorcycle, with a very hard pillion seat. There was every prospect of my becoming an early widow, as Kay had been in France since early nineteen-fifteen. But though I was only twenty-two years old, we had already been courting for seven years, and engaged off and on for three of them.

I see people marrying today. I see them looking as if they are really delighted with each other. They marry, and the strangest things happen to them. They go away for a honeymoon, and come back to their nicely feathered nests, and begin the process of settling down to a new life, with varying results. Sometimes they grow comfortably dull, and sometimes they begin to dislike each other pretty soon. It is nice — and rare — to meet an interesting young married couple.

What it was that impelled me to marriage, I do not

know. This is the truth, that I do not know. I was used to Kay, I knew that he thought I was much nicer than I was, and nobody else had asked me. I had read of love, but dismissed it in my ignorance, thinking it was an imaginary thing, like heaven. For years, I turned my cheek for kisses, and it was not a bad sort of life at all. When I was due for a lesson, I got it. And perhaps I have learned something about marriage in the end.

We can laugh now about our honeymoon, but it did not seem so funny then. It was the middle of a very cold winter, when spirits were at their lowest ebb. The war had been on for more than three years, and seemed likely to go on for ever. I had spent five of my husband's precious twenty-five pounds on a trousseau, investing it fairly sensibly in a white blanket coat, a pair of clomping boots — which I used for getting married in — some woollen underclothes, and one extravagance — a couple of embroidered cotton nightdresses, one pink-ribboned, and the other blue. Underneath my wedding coat, I wore my ordinary grey tweed office skirt, and a white satin blouse, and black woollen stockings. I had also a befrilled white hat, which I had bought cheap at a sale. I must have looked extraordinarily comic, but nobody told me so.

We were married by a pathetic-looking little curate with a cold, who went to his lonely bed and died of influenza soon afterwards. There was no wedding feast. No wedding cakes were being made at that time — or if there were any, one would have been far beyond our means. There were no flowers and no music. As I walked up the aisle, I wondered what on earth I was doing, and if Kay felt as silly as I did. The ring was too small for my finger, and the parson stopped the service to say in an agonized voice, 'Wet it, wet it!'

I remember stumping along to the vestry, and hearing my boots squeak in a loud yet reverential way, as if they knew they were in church, and the occasion was important. Somebody called me Mrs Whitaker, and I flinched, not liking the name. But I realized, though my wedding day was both dull and ridiculous, that I liked my husband in a friendly way, and that he liked me, too. We were glad to get away together.

The motorcycle was wrapped against the winter frosts, so we went to Morecambe by train. Although we had first-class tickets — for the first time in our lives — and were sure we should be alone, an insensitive old man carrying a large cheese got in our compartment. As the journey progressed, and the coach grew warmer, the cheese began to smell very powerfully. The train stopped at many stations, but we were too polite to find another carriage away from the old man and his cheese, and the train was an old-fashioned one, without a corridor, so we got our first lesson in making the best of things.

It did not take us long to become used to each other. The only physical result of our union was that I was left with the itch, which complaint was very rife in the army, though never mentioned in the popular novels of the period, and it took much time and many sulphur baths to get rid of it. I shall never forget that awful period of retiring to dark corners for a mad orgy of scratching. Fortunately I gave it to my sister, and we were able to scratch in anguished company.

Nowadays, people are working in a very lively way for the cause of Peace. All honour to them. A 'promoted' war is a rotten thing, and it seems to me that there can now be no other kind. I can understand the old idea of going out to fight hand to hand for glory, adventure, and profit. But the sordid business of the war of nineteen-fourteen — when it was upon us — can never be forgotten by those who lived through it. We were really persuaded that other human beings were wicked, and our enemies. (Those of us who were young, I mean. The others ought to have had more sense.) The only thing I felt was sorrow and loneliness. I also felt that I was a kind of miserable traitor when I barred the bathroom door and wept behind it because a Zeppelin had fallen blazing from the sky.

Kay used to come home on leave, and quietly tell me stories of ordinary and human things he had seen in France; queer, touching stories, of French and Germans, and Belgians; even of a Chinese in one of the Labour Corps. He told of his own part in the Christmas fraternizing with the so-called enemy. Oh! the thing is unbearable to think of. The organized killing and maiming, when there was only good feeling between man and man, until a streak of power or evil got between them. Pray God the young will never let themselves be hoodwinked again. We, the foolish, had to live through it. We were not trained in revolt. The power was turned on, and we were caught in the machine — shot whether we enlisted or deserted; and nobody noticed the sacrifice in any case.

Six months after the war, my husband was demobilized. We spent a month at home. I was in a job, so we lived. But the world was a changing place. Life was one mad scramble for jobs, and we didn't like the look of things.

There was the war gratuity, which seemed large to us, and was the biggest sum of money we had ever possessed. We were young, but at the same time old. Our real youth had gone in those four hellish years. We had had the feeling for so long that the next moment might be the last that we had no thought about money except to spend it.

We packed what odd clothes we had, and bought two single tickets to Rouen. We got a cheap furnished room at the top of a tall old house in the rue St Patrice, and there we stayed until our money was spent.

For the last six months we lived entirely on bread and tomatoes, having only one dinner during the whole of that time — a treat given by a friend who happened to meet us. He had made a great deal of money at home during the war, and ordered champagne for me to drink. Real food tasted quite strange.

Kay kept trying his hand at odd spots of business, and we almost got to the point of opening a small office in our own street. We got to know a fat, asthmatic Frenchman who said that all English birds were called Tim-tots, and who would wave his hand and say 'So far, so far', when we parted. We went to Paris, and walked from end to end of it, but did not spend a single penny there; yet we saw every free sight.

On my twenty-fourth birthday, our landlady astonished me by giving me a bouquet of flowers. I had never been given any flowers in my life before that, so I astonished her by crying heartily on her shoulder. She had two married daughters in England, and was apt to mother me. I accepted her bounty with the thoughtlessness of the young, and am only now conscious of her generosity.

Her remaining daughters took a shower-bath once a fortnight in some public baths, but she confided to me that she had never had a bath in her life. Conscious of some lack, she passed it off with a kind of confused airiness, but she had a pleasanter smell than many well-bathed people I have known.

Of course, the time came when we had to go back. France's troubles were starting. The franc fell from twenty-eight to sixty-eight in a few hours. One of Kay's business deals had really come off, and he bought tickets for London. I can't say that I wanted very much to go back; but that part of life was past, and at that time, everything in the world seemed to be before us.

I got a job immediately, in the share department of a large limited company. My handwriting was quite good, and I loved to write shares. If I have lived before, I think I was once a monk who copied manuscripts. I am nearly sure that I have often been on this earth before, and even in this country.

When I had accidentally collected three pounds — I could never have saved it, but it came into my possession somehow — we bought an old green belltent, and hired the corner of a field for a shilling a week. My mother gave us an ancient iron bedstead, and that and a box or two and a paraffin stove completed our furniture. We enjoyed living in that tent. Our worst moments were when it rained, for the tent leaked everywhere. We were sorry for the man who had sold it to us. I always feel pity for people who live by sharp practice; they are liable to be overtaken by terrible remorse when it is too late to do anything about it but suffer.

There was another bad moment, when a young cow tossed me, and hurt my leg rather badly. It sounds heroic to say you have been tossed by a bull but I never succumbed to the temptation of lying about it. This was a cow with a very strong head and red eyes. When it came close and began looking at me, I saw that it had the sullen appearance of a misunderstood creature, so I said 'Nice cow, nice cow', in a conciliatory tone. It took no notice of my overtures, but pressed its head closer and closer into my side. I screamed, as the cow was on my left, and a very hard stone wall was on my right. The farmer's wife afterwards said to me, 'I just thought it was a pig', so I must have screamed on the wrong note. The cow tossed me over the wall, so I was saved.

After that, we lived in various places — in people's weekend cottages, miles away from anywhere, in rooms at a farmhouse, in an attic at home. Then came the great day when we really rented a house! We removed in a milk float. By this time, we had some blankets, a washing tub, a bed and a table, and some wooden chairs. I put all the soft furnishings in the wash-tub, and rode on the top of it, singing in the autumn twilight. I was twenty-six, my husband had got a good job, and I was determined to be a housewife at last.

We didn't like it. We threw up this, our first home, to go and live in somebody's summer bungalow on the moors beyond Ilkley. It was grand to get up early, and be there, high and lonely, just when our part of the world was waking too. The fire had to be lit before breakfast could be made, and water had to be fetched from a spring across the field; and there were times when it must have rained, and hailed, and snowed. But I can't recall those. Every morning I walked down with Kay to the station, just over two miles away, saw him off on the train, bought my groceries in the village, and climbed back again.

The rent was only half a crown a week. And every time we had a holiday and some money, we went as far as the money could take us. It took us three days' continuous travel to get from Paris to Lisbon, but there was hardly an hour without its thrill. We got stuck in a tunnel in the middle of Spain. The driver of this slow train had not got enough steam up to take the rise. It grew hotter and hotter — this was during a September heatwave — and the people in the carriage gradually discarded most of their clothing. We were all bleeding slowly at the nose when the train moved at last. But at least it had been a change.

When we had been married nine years, we built a

small house. This turned out to be on the site of an ancient British village, and we dug a perfect quern up in the garden. The place was on the shoulder of a hill, and was free and lonely. But soon houses grew up all around, and we left that place, too.

But I wrote my first book of stories there, and most of my second. Editors began to buy them, a fact which astonished me then, and still astonishes me. It is now four years since I wrote a word, but still the stories keep on being printed. And for this, I am grateful.

10

This morning, I seem to be on the verge of some great discovery. The sun is so bright and yellow, and it shines across one gently-moving spider-thread which has attached itself to either side of a window. Each leaf on each tree is separate and impressed against its background. Baby has come in to tell me some story which I cannot understand. Her hand gently touches me, and her large eyes, full of sincerity, fix themselves on mine.

If I have any immediate worries, they have mellowed or withdrawn themselves. Our wild garden, with its rapidly growing grass, looks attractive to me, but I like to be inside the house rather than out. I cannot read in a sunny garden, nor do much work. It is altogether too bright and dreamy. Every time a breeze stirs the air it alters the appearance of everything, and I must look at the change. I had rather think of a garden as a place of rest than use it as one.

It is baking day. We have kept milk until it has turned into a solid jelly, and the yellow bowl is warming in the sunshine, with half a stone of flour in it. We always bake our own bread. There are few lovelier smells than that of baking bread. I am not a very good baker, myself, though I can do it. I haven't got the genuine touch. I find myself thinking of other things when I am kneading, and flour only responds to loving treatment.

In the garden, away from the house, stands an old stable, part of which is now the garage, the doors of which are perpetually open, because the rump of our new M.G. sticks out inelegantly. Over the stable is a loft, with wooden steps running up to it. I had it cleaned and made into a playroom for the children, and fixed a swing for them, and took out their larger toys. But they never used the room, so I had it cleared again, and made it into a kind of hideout for myself. And now *I* never use it, though I go over sometimes to sweep the moths and dust from the windowsills.

It is a long, wide room, with coconut matting on the floor, a couple of desks, a divan, a chair and a round table. It is furnished with household throwouts. The desks are only comic. I have never used one. There are half a dozen windows in the room, which look out over as many hills.

Sometimes I think of the last occupant of the room — an old farm labourer who ended his days in it. But his spirit, if he has one, is calm and peaceful. I remember his thin face, with its bright, consumptive colour, his sandy moustache, and his slow, nasal voice. He came, worked at the farm for a number of years, and then died. He must have opened the door in the garden wall, over which is carved T.W. 1627, trudged past the side of the house, and climbed the wooden stairway to his lonely bed each night.

Yes, I have too much, when a man's whole earthly home is merely a playroom to me.

I have come over to my room after all. The farmer's wife paid me a visit yesterday, and told me that old William did not die here. I am both glad and sorry. I would not mind dying in a room like this, with the wind straight from the moors howling around.

She said, 'He only had a beetriss to keep him warm. He wore I don't know how many shirts.' So old William has become more alive to me than ever, for I don't know what a beetriss is, though I imagine it is a paraffin stove. There are times when I am sure I could live here, in solitude.

No, that is not true. I love solitude occasionally, but more often I love the company of my fellow-men. Of course, we all live in complete solitude. It is hardly possible to have real contact with another human being. When I have thought I have had it, I have been wrong. We are blind, and deaf, and speechless, even though a tower of Babel was built, and we still live in it. But like the alleged inhabitants of Mars, we are always trying to get through to each other, with the strangest results.

I have come to the conclusion that I know nothing. I do not know what will be happening to me within five minutes of the thing we call time, therefore how dare I say I have even a faint intuition? I expect I shall grow hungry, and have lunch at the usual hour. Yet I do not know. And the things behind me, things like painfully-acquired arithmetic, are strange to me, and not of much use. Reading flows in and out of me like breath; it is something to keep my mind alive, as oxygen and — I have forgotten what else — keeps alive my body. I like to read what other people have written, in the hope that I can get a glimpse of the garden enclosed, through a tiny peephole.

For I do believe that everybody owns the equivalent of a garden; a place inside themselves that they know has something really good in it; something from which they can give. But the flowers have a habit of turning to the rankest weeds during the transfer.

My husband read the marriage chapter of this journal. Every now and then he said, 'You shouldn't say this', or 'You mustn't say this', or 'You'll have to cut this out'. So this is how truth is shorn of a fingernail, and then an eye, a nose, an ear, until presently you can't see the poor thing at all.

Yesterday, I spent a long time gardening, for the second time in my life; or for the second time since I was four. In my childhood, we used sometimes to have an old jobbing gardener, also called William, and he would let me help him. But once he shared his lunch with me. It was called 'roice poy', and made me very sick, and perhaps that kept me from the land for almost thirty-eight years.

How wonderful it is now I have started! I knew it was working in me when I began to think up schemes for circumventing the autumn rains. There were too many trees, and too much twitch-grass. And nothing would be better than to have the courtyard as a court-yard. There are old stone hitching-posts in it, and now we have torn off the twitch-grass and dug a foot deep, we find that there was once a cobbled courtyard. We are covering that up with stone flags from the quarries which stand almost at our doors. Cobbles are pic-turesque but treacherous, and they hold pools of water.

I don't know what is making me think there will be a lot of rain this autumn. But I do. We are still in August. There is sunlight and wind. Because of all the autumns behind me, I can visualize still another, with its savage wind and its bitter, pelting rain. How well I know the prolonged sound of water which steadily overflows from a gutter, and the almost human groan-ing of old trees creaking under the gale. When I read the description of a storm, I think suddenly, 'There *must* be something alike in every one of us. We can feel this wind and this rain. We have the same urge to battle against it, and win through in the end'.

And win through in the end. But to what?

There are people who come here and say to us, 'Why have you done all that work when it's not your house?' It is true that we do not own the house, we pay rent for it. But my mind is not filled with answers. I do not know why we do things except that we want to do them. To do things for some definite reason is not my strong point. We have what is called 'made provision' for the children; but even that seems a kind of indulgent silliness to me. I hope we shall still be alive when they are old enough to look after themselves, and that they will live to look on money as a means and not an end.

No, money is a funny thing. I spend mine in my own way, as does everybody else. Nearly all my life, I have lived that little bit beyond my income which makes for pure happiness. I can, and do, the more enjoy those things which I know I ought not to have — the little extra things with the tang of forbidden fruit in them. How horrible it would be if all the nights were calm and peaceful with security! If one need never raise frightened eyes to a blank, black ceiling and wonder where the next money is coming from; and fall asleep exhausted with thinking, and wake full of hope and ambition. Or so it has happened to me, many a time. And I only know that things do turn up — though never if I expect them, and never in the way I have anticipated. An astrologically-minded friend assures me that I am protected by Jupiter. If that is so, I can recommend Jupiter, wholeheartedly, as a protector.

I can put forward no reason for the intense happiness that sometimes fills me. Or if there is one, it is my sense of gratitude. I do not believe that I am grateful to God, the Church of England or even the Chapel (Hellfire) God to whom I was introduced in early childhood. And unfortunately I do not know any others, except in an off-hand way. I don't want to worship anything, I want to love it, but I don't know what love is any more than I know what life is, or time, or death.

No, I am filled with gratitude because of the way human beings can suddenly and for no known reason spontaneously give away all the best in themselves and still remain in no way depleted; and for the way in which one is allowed now and then to receive. It is very hard to accept graciously — or at least, the thought of it is hard, but it is like any other strange happening in life; when the moment is upon you, so is the revelation. It is all a matter of the flame being applied. And that, I think, is why I am so fond of fire. Fire exists, and happiness is a kind of fire.

It has taken me many and bitter years to reject from my mind the things that were given to it in the early years. I retain strong impressions of ordinary life — being the eighth of eleven children — being loved by my mother, pushed about and trodden on by my brothers, tolerated by my sisters, and gradually fighting my way into the outside world. I found it strange, and I couldn't believe it. There was hypocrisy, which even put its ugly face in our home, though not often. There was lying, which I could understand and forgive. But I couldn't forgive the way I wanted spiritual bread and was always being given stones.

I had — I still have a disconcerting eye. It doesn't see through things so easily now, but it did then. I should like to know if anybody gets real bread, or if we must live on a diet of stones, all of us.

The farmer's wife often talks to me. She is sure of certain things, for which she has names, like Redeemer, and The Lamb, and Precious Blood. She says that if I keep on looking for the truth, I shall find it. But some truths don't smell right to me.

Ecclesiastes says 'Better is the sight of the eyes than the wandering of desire.'

That may be true, but it won't work in everyday life. The eyes light upon unpleasant things, and the wandering of desire can be very beautiful. Of course, there may be a catch in it somewhere. These prophets wouldn't have stood so long if they hadn't had something behind them. And that something might be a double meaning that I in my ignorance miss. Here is the man who said 'If the iron be blunt, and he do not whet the edge, then must he put to more strength: but wisdom is profitable to direct'. Could this be a translation? 'Some men have more brawn than brains; but if you've got knowledge, keep it to line your pocket.'

I am glad it was a scribe who said to Christ: Which is the first commandment of all?

And Christ answered him, The first of all the commandments is Hear O Israel; The Lord our God is one Lord:

And thou shalt love the Lord thy God with all thy heart, and with all thy soul, and with all thy mind, and with all thy strength: this is the first commandment.

And the second is like, namely this, Thou shalt love thy neighbour as thyself. There is none other commandment greater than these.

I have never understood this before. I was right to think this morning that I was on the verge of a discovery. It is the best-sounding advice I have ever read. But in practice it is next door to impossible. You can start it all right, but what follows? People begin to demand things from you, not just material things, but your time, and your patience, and inexhaustible love. And suddenly you have to say with the man in Gissing's novel *The Unclassed*, 'I can no more. I have done my possible.'

It is better to have too much work than too little. I know that is a platitude, but platitudes are so true that I am amazed that people do not talk in them more. There is one person with whom I can play that game for ten minutes at a time. We can carry on long conversations about it taking all sorts to make a world, and how I always say there's nothing like a nice cup of tea. All the same, I will repeat that it is better to have too much work than too little.

This is the ninth day of housework for me. I loathe housework, because I am compelled to do it too well. I must get into corners, and scrub behind objects, instead of gracefully sliding past the outsides and forgetting them, as so many people do who take on the job and are paid for it.

I like money. It is a fluid thing. I like to earn it. But passionately I like to earn it well. And I feel both sick and sorry when in my own house I find things mouldering in corners. This means that somebody has done work badly, and taken money for doing it; which is exactly the same as stealing. My policy, which has never yet turned out well, is to trust people. I tell them at the beginning that I trust them. But only one has been really worthy of that trust, and she couldn't be trained. She would pursue dirt from morning to night with a smile and a song; she never saw ordinary untidiness, and she had no idea of time. But somehow she suited us. And now she is married, and producing child after child, like a queen bee, giving them really romantic names. She was there when we brought Nick home, and helped us through many a whooping crisis.

It is good to have every minute filled. Yesterday I roasted a fillet of lamb for dinner, and we had it with mint sauce and garden potatoes and peas. My sister said, 'You look *just right* basting that joint'. As last year my friend said I looked just right picking fruit in a garden. I am descended from people who scratched a bare living farming on the moors, and it surprises me that I write at all. I can't join clubs or go to authors' dinners or give lectures. All that seems a different world to me, and one that I don't hanker for. For my type, there's sufficient here.

I think, when I see an old countrywoman in a sun-bonnet and an ample cotton gown hobbling along with the help of a stick, that here is myself as I shall soon be. Even now, after many lovely things, I am at last looking forward to an old age where the body's problems become little by little harder, and the mind — poor, feverish, blown out thing — retreats to some inner fastness in readiness for the sea–change.

11

Today is the last day of the working fortnight. It has been a sanative experience. This is not one of the words I know. I have just learnt it. It means healing.

It seems to me that the house and garden look better for the rest from paid labour; freer, more windblown. It seems to me also that I have come out of years of inertia. Can this all be the result of a surgical operation? For three years I had written no stories. Of course, the children were there to look after, but there are women who can bring up children with one hand and write very long novels with the other. I simply felt lazy, and suddenly couldn't do either.

I consulted a specialist, and soon after that, found myself on an operating table, being remoulded nearer to the heart's desire. The whole of this last operation was one great pleasure, except for the supper of poached egg on spinach which I had to eat the first night I entered the nursing home. I certainly did not like that, but I had made up my mind to place myself in the hands of people who knew much more about internal organs than I did.

What is there about ether which makes people afraid? If you make up your mind to enjoy an experience, whatever it is, you can usually get something very funny out of it. And I got a lot of fun out of this. I had had ether before, but never with the prospect of three weeks of unadulterated bed in a pleasant nursing home in front of me.

In this place, they have a practice of putting you to sleep in your own room, and then wheeling you down the corridor to the operating theatre. I climbed on to a stretcher bed, and lay on it, watching things with interest. Of course, nurses and doctors must get terribly used to operations, but they can never get blasé. There's something about the job which prevents boredom.

I lay perfectly relaxed, and surrendered myself to the laughter and jokes of the anaesthetist. It is not difficult to 'go under' ether. Only the mind makes it so. I wanted to get into the blackness, so that this day and the next few could be finished with. Then there would be something to look forward to. So I vanished quietly, and knew nothing until I woke up in my bed again.

I suppose the next day or two were bad ones. I was allowed to wet my tongue with water, but not to drink. And I wanted to drink. How I wanted to drink! My mind made the most delectable pictures. I thought of every lovely thing I had ever drunk in my life; I saw lemons and oranges growing in clusters, and stretched out my hands for them. I crushed the juice from great bunches of grapes until I felt it running down my chin. But the time was passing, bringing me nearer and nearer to an almost perfect health.

The following fortnight was pure joy. I had never stayed in bed so long before since I was a child. There was time to think, and to read. Flowers mean nothing at all to me — unless they are a reminder of death, for the poor things are slowly and visibly dying from the minute they are picked, and only trouble me — so I had none in the room. And that seemed to amuse the surgeon. He lent me books on the ballet, and told me that he always spent his holidays in Switzerland, climbing. Is it possible that this man's life is divided into three compartments — for I have talked to him often, and he will not tell me of any more — operating on people, climbing mountains, and watching the ballet. No, it is not possible.

I knew that that time was a pleasant backwater in life, and that I was needed back on the job. So I went home, and learned to walk again. There were so many stitches inside me that I felt I could never stand upright again. And the long scar has faded to the mauve-white colour of the flower we call the milkmaid; as to my mind, there was no scar left at all, there.

I have just finished reading another of those books about Soviet Russia. It was even more self-consciously dreary than most. The land, Russia, cannot be different. Most of the people cannot be different. Communism only reminds me of the difference I used to feel between school and home. School was filled with useless and unnecessary organizing; games must be played, sums must be done, words must be spelled. And what poor creatures the schools spew out.

The *idea* of Communism is a fearful and wonderful one; just as ants must have been to their creator. And bees, too. But I would rather die than live helping to make everything one uniform level. I like to work now and then, but not all the time. I had rather work less than more. And I am also greedy. I would rather have enough of something, once, than stingy driblets for the rest of my life. But perhaps that is not greed, but good, sound sense.

I am glad I live in England, and not in Russia, for I love being here, and I love enjoying those things which I suppose are nothing, but which seem to me to have taken a long time to earn. And I am glad I have had more than a nodding acquaintance with luck — the greatest of these — as well as love and some depths of human understanding in my fellow-creatures. You cannot *possess* anything here, but once you find that out, a milestone is passed.

Of the two evils, Fascism seems to me more repulsive than Communism. I don't want to do anything to quantities of other people. I want to begin with myself. But not today. Christ was right, after all, to give us impossible ideals, yet ideals that we can strive for — to subdue our evil — no, not evil, our silly — passions; and to give out love. I would like to love my neighbour as myself, because I have a warm, passionate, and forgiving love for myself, which I should like to spread through the whole universe, instead of keeping it for myself alone.

I am one of the teeming millions who do not want either Fascism or Communism. We will be neither led nor driven, because we are slow to think, and don't want to have our thoughts broken into and rifled. But we are here, as the grass is here.

Is there a single-minded man? The 'God' man in the hospital, perhaps. He came over to my sister the other day, as she sat beside my father, and told her that he had been able to bring even more sweets and tobacco to the old men because of my ten shillings. 'And you should have seen their smiles!' he said. My sister likes him and is angry when I attempt to explain him pathologically. But I can only wonder why the patients smile more for four sweets than for two. It isn't the pleasure of the man's company, or his self-sacrifice, that they appreciate. No, it's the augmented toffees. *He* gets pleasure out of their smiles, and *they* get pleasure out of the sweets. But where does God come in?

After many disappointing thunderstorms, a steady rain has arrived to stay. The children, in the way of children kept in by rain, have been hitting each other over the heads with fishing rods, knocking down each other's bricks, tormenting each other with toy balloons, and — when all else in the way of amusement failed — howling drearily in different keys. Now is the time for me to rush in and organize something, get them interested, start a mass movement, even introduce folk-dancing or fol-de-rol a bit. But I sit here where I am. I think that this is life, and that they are being educated in it. They may remember this rainy afternoon as a time which had all heaven in it, only they did not know.

Autumn arrived this morning — early and unofficially. I looked out of the window to see the cows standing motionless in the farmyard, while the first fallen leaves drifted around their hooves. There was a faint smell of smoke blown downwards, and a migrating bird was hopping foolishly round and round a patch of earth — foolishly, because it did not know about the cunning farm cats, and I did. I wish it would get on with its migrating.

The house has gone back to normal. I opened my eyes to morning tea and Delia's cheerful morning face — not so cheerful as usual, because she has not been well for the whole of her holiday. Delia is the younger of the two maids. She went to Yarmouth, but had to leave it after a few days, and go back to her home. I feel both worried and sorry, but it may only be love. She spends all her spare time in the cinema, and has drawn the sad, pictured lives to her heart, so that she does not distinguish reality from dreams. If I speak to her suddenly, she jerks into the present like an animated doll, starting, frowning and smiling all at once, anxious to please, because we like each other, but pulled from some distant, hazy shore, where faces are yards long, and where every strand of hair and every eyelash is a thick, soft rope. I cannot think what her fate will be, but I hope a happy one is in store for her, as she is very gentle.

'Shall I take this away?' she asks.

She always asks my advice about anything lying about. 'This', happens to be a broken gramophone record. Last night, a jinny-spinner (the local name for daddy-long-legs) was zooming about the room. It kept getting in my hair, and once or twice I sprang up with a loud yell, because I do not like mysterious buzzings near my ear. And this insect was abnormal, for it had a kind of long, black boot on. When it was near the oak beam which crosses the ceiling, my husband threw the *Amateur Gardening Year Book* at it. He missed the prey, but the year book caught the record on its way down.

I wish I could grow good enough to live and let live. When I feel happy, I cannot bear to brush the tiniest life away. I look at flies with a benign expression, and have even invented a way to get wasps out of the window. All that is necessary is a glass tumbler and a strong picture postcard. Put the tumbler over the wasp as it crawls angrily up the window-pane, and slip the postcard under the rim. Go outside, withdraw the card, and away the wasp flies. It always seems to realize that it has had a narrow escape, and gets away as quickly as a human being from an unpleasant situation.

There has been a plague of moths this year, and unfortunately moths are terribly easy to kill. If you merely brush them, they come to pieces in your hand. It is a pity that their mother instinct invariably leads them to the best blankets. One can't feel affection for fat white worms with black heads which have already eaten their way through some treasured garment. It is always too late to do anything when they are found. I suppose the real solution is not to have anything hoarded away. I have bought enough lavender this year to stun every moth I have seen. But perhaps they like lavender?

Today, I should like to be a hermit. What an easy time the saints must have had! When we read about them and their sufferings, we do seem to forget that their agonies were their delight. They were perpetually sustained on clouds of joy, and only had genuine suffering when doubts gnawed them. I think it must be much harder to be an ordinary man who has married a woman and begotten some children, and then finds he has made a mistake, and yet sets his teeth and stands by and provides for them. Much, much harder! The would-be saints had only to fast, and lash themselves into a frenzy to dispose of their doubts. What fun it must have been to have had nothing to keep at bay but the devil!

There are so many more people now, and life is less easy and less spectacular. The patient, steady setting of oneself to do a task and doing it is much harder than leaving human troubles behind, and going away to meditate. The lovely word 'meditate' reminds me of a drawing I saw thirty years ago, in which a couple were speaking to a sexton in a churchyard. 'I suppose people often come here to meditate.' The sexton answers 'That they do! I caught two of 'em at it last week.'

To have nobody but oneself to please! To have most of one's wants supplied by people who come to see the 'holy man'! To be lost in mystical communion with a sure and certain God! What a strange way of living!

No, it gets harder the more I think of it. I want to know things, but I cannot believe that the way to wisdom is by intensive study. With such study, there is a tendency to forget everything else. Specialists in anything are wearisome unless they have an all-round understanding as well, and they very rarely have. King Charles's head comes into all they do — no, they drag it in; and there it squats blandly to their satisfaction and my dismay.

I can't help liking the Bible, because it is clear and simple. I find my problem all over it, but not the solution.

'If thou wouldst seek unto God betimes, and make thy supplication to the Almighty.

'If thou wert pure and upright; surely now would he awake for thee, and make the habitation of thy righteousness prosperous.'

But I cannot pray. It makes me feel as if I were drinking from an empty glass, and eating from an empty plate. And God won't awake for me, because I am not pure and upright, and I can never become so, unless this happens without my knowledge, say if I should be paralysed.

Bildad the Shuhite says to Job:

'Can the rush grow up without mire? can the flag grow without water?

'Whilst it is yet in his greenness, and not cut down, it withereth before any other herb.

'So are the paths of all that forget God; and the hypocrite's hope shall perish:

'Whose hope shall be cut off, and whose trust shall be a spider's web.

'He shall lean upon his house, but it shall not stand: he shall hold it fast, but it shall not endure.'

But what use is all this? I have been carried away by sweet-sounding words — rush and mire, flag and water, greenness and withereth. I don't forget God, and if I am a hypocrite, it is an unconscious one. Perhaps there is some vital thing lacking in me. I can't shoot up like a short-lived flame in vivid enthusiasms or dislikes. For people who say 'When I see a man ill-treating a poor, dumb beast, I could beat him until he drops!' I have a faint, passing contempt. When I read of the hatred of others for 'growing suburbia' I have the same slightly-tinged tolerance. There is ugliness in warped minds, but not so much in newly-built houses, which in the words of others 'spoil the countryside'. The countryside can take them without complaint, and in a very little while as we know it, can turn them into things of beauty by throwing over them a mantle of grass, and trees, and eventually quiet dust. Patience, patience! Is that what is needed?

'Better is the end of a thing than the beginning thereof: and the patient in spirit is better than the proud in spirit.'

That's a good thought in the search for God. I will try to become patient in spirit. Another impossibility. Patience is too near stupidity, and many a time I feel myself to be stupid like a cow or a pig or a mule. No, not a mule, for that is thin and delicate, and not a pig, for the pig is too soft and its eyes are too small. I am stupid like a cow. Oh, that I had the power to turn grass and water into milk. But it is not in me.

12

The peace of Sunday was suddenly ripped by the ringing of the telephone bell. As this noise only occurs two or three times a week, and never on Sundays, I ran towards the sound with an anticipatory heart. An abrupt male voice asked for my house-maid. Possibly because it was male, I rushed off to find Delia, but could only find Fan, the red-haired girl who cooks for us between the intervals of reading the film weeklies.

I could not help hearing what she said, as I was most interestedly listening. Fan came out of the room shining-eyed to tell me that Delia's young man had ridden over from Doncaster on his bicycle, and would it be all right if she met him when she took baby for her afternoon walk.

My heart always melts for young love, so I said, 'Bring him back to tea with you'. Baby decided at the top of her voice that she would not go for a walk, that all she wished for was her parents' company. So she stayed at home while the girls went to meet Henry.

Henry has come in the plural. There are three of him, all on bicycles, and all hungry. Luckily there is the new baking of bread, and yesterday's joint of beef. I can't help liking the way Delia came to me for advice, or being glad that I can say 'Make them some sandwiches'. I love people to have food, especially in a strange place when they are hungry.

Nicholas could not keep away from the three Henrys, though the three Henrys did not find the abiding joy in his presence that I do. So I have asked him to stay with me. These are easy words, but it was not an easy thing to make him do. One has to explain things to children nowadays, but the textbooks never go on to say what you must do when the child will not accept your explanations. I don't like to whack him — I don't know why. Perhaps he would be better for it. My mother was a believer in corporal punishment, and I can't think of any harm it has done any member of the family. But she had a lot more children and many other things to put up with which I haven't; and we seemed to know that her flashing hand was an outlet for her wounded feelings, and loved her none the less for her sharp smacks.

So I asked him — just a shade casually — to look up the word 'bicycle' in the dictionary. I knew there was a y in it, but was not sure just where. He has never looked in a dictionary before, and was entranced by it, going from 'bicentenary' to 'bicker' and so on to 'biffins', which are apples slowly dried in bakers' ovens and flattened into cakes — prepared in great quantities in Norfolk, said to be properly beefins, because like raw beef, a fact entirely new to me.

In spite of my early hospitable thoughts, the three Henrys stayed too long, and ate too much. My hospitality was really for one Henry; it was a delicate thing, which pined away under the onslaught of ninety-six chewing teeth, and died long before their owners borrowed a flashlight because one of their number had no lamp, and sailed spectacularly away on their bicycles, to the accompaniment of loud and cheerful laughter and conversation from the girls.

But the day had its compensations, for my husband had brought a couple of Penguin books back with him to read in the train, and they turned out to be *Some Experiences of a New Guinea Resident Magistrate* — two volumes filled with half a lifetime of adventure. They make me feel like a pet rabbit. They also rouse the strangest thoughts in me. Why must we ram our so-called civilization down the throats of people for whom it is utterly unfitted?

Cannibalism must be dying out now, but I have often thought that if I had to choose between that and starvation, I should plump for cannibalism every time, and have no sickly shame about it. Perhaps I should be a little finicky, preferring the joints only, even if they were a bit tough; or soup; but I could not touch brains or kidney or liver or sweetbreads (if humans possess these things) as I can never stand them from animals.

I like to think of some child of the future poring over these books — stories of things which have happened during my own lifetime — which have completely enthralled me. I do not like the people who are always complaining that the days of adventure are dead. What could they think when a modest voice came not so long ago out of the ether, describing a journey to the stratosphere which had that morning broken a record? I knew that I was living in an age of miracles.

We are luckier today than ever in the pursuit of adventure for its own sake. In other days, lives were thrown away wholesale, but today one man and one machine can compass wonders.

The doctor called today. He has just returned from his holidays. He looked over the children, made one or two of his oracular comments, and gave me half a dozen exercises to perform. I am getting worried about the way I ripple when I stand up and sit down. The surgeon has overshot his mark, and made me too well. I am going to town next week, and a BBC man has asked me to lunch, because he has read some of my stories and thinks I might write something more for him. This lunch will be eaten on false pretences, as I do not intend to write a word for the BBC. I think most things that are read are colossally dull, and I cannot bear to add to the number of boring hours. But I do not want to carry an ungainly-looking stomach to the meal, however efficient it is in other ways. Something has got to be done.

There are plenty of funny things to be seen. Houses are being built still nearer and nearer. They have got some opposite the chapel itself, now. Yesterday, when I passed, three of the husky workmen were standing in the open doorway of a half-built house, talking to a roundsman, and drinking pints of milk from the wide-mouthed glass bottles. It looked like some skit on the stage. Yet in my heart, I suppose they will be better for drinking milk than beer.

When a man has done some particularly hard manual labour for us in the house or garden (or men, if you count the time when the house was on fire) I always say, 'Would like you a drink . . . of tea . . . or beer?' I say it very slowly, so that they have the choice. But I find it comes out about half and half. There are confirmed tea-drinkers among men. And there were two original plumbers — a father and son — who preferred a glass of sherry. Some ask diffidently for water. There is a wicked way to take all pleasure out of beer — and that is to serve it on a tray with a dainty cloth and a mock-Jacobean glass, and one bottle of a well-advertised brand standing hard and proud like a grim old lady.

When I am really hungry and thirsty, I like half a pint of bitter in a quiet pub, town or country, a chunk of bread one and a half to two inches thick, and a lump of cheese out of which I can pick the middle; drunk and eaten at a table so well scrubbed that it sinks in the middle like a butcher's block. This has only happened about a dozen times in my life, but each time has been so good that I remember it with pleasure. There are odd pubs, the pictures of which rise like visions of heaven in my remembering mind. I knew that I was happy then, and I know it now. Gratitude for life is about to overwhelm me again, I fear. A spring of joy has come in the place of my banished appendix.

Sticky oilcloth-and-fly pubs are my pet abomination. Ambition is dead in them, and there is no filthier sight anywhere than dead ambition. It lies stinking and rotting away, never getting down to clean bones. Pubs are rather like human beings — except, of course, there are fewer of them.

Last night when my husband and I were gardening, and the incomparable English twilight was falling with the utmost gentleness over town and countryside, we heard the sound of a car, and knew that we had a rare visitor. The road leading to the house is only a track, and there is a sudden sharp turn into the farm gate, and a lunge forward into the farmyard. Then our own gates appear, and our beautiful, secret house.

We like this man's company for no particular known reason. We have only had his acquaintance for eighteen months, but we shall never know him better than we do now. Life has trained him to pretend to talk, and to tell funny stories and interesting experiences. But he never really says anything. He doesn't mind you knowing the top layer of his thoughts, and sometimes, on occasion, the second. But the rest (if there is any more) is his own. He is very hearty. Sometimes I want to say, 'You needn't be like that here. We aren't going to hurt you.' And he loves poetry.

During my convalescence a few months ago, he gave me a copy of his favourite book of poems. To me, a present is a wonderful thing, so much so, that I hate to receive one, as a rule. My generosity is the easy kind. I give because I am possessed by the desire to give at that moment, and then I forget about it immediately. Sometimes I look quite dense when I am thanked for something I have so forgotten.

These poems touched a part of the youth that is still left in me, for they are made of the essence of youth. But the idea of the present touched me far more. I realized that I had been given more than a volume of poems. The man had cast his pearl before a swine. I am a swine, for the author of the poems is no pearl to me. I am ashamed. I have not been worthy of the gift. There must be something false in me which made the man think I should love his poet.

That is how it goes with presents. We all get the wrong things and we all give the wrong things. We should perhaps make presents only to ourselves. My husband now knows enough to ask me what I want for my birthday, and twice I have had to reply agonizedly, 'I don't know. I don't really want anything'.

When well-dressed husbands in films bring their wives bracelets (it always seems to be diamond bracelets) or necklaces for their wedding anniversaries, tears come into the eyes of the wives, and they act as if they are really pleased. I have never known anybody do this in real life. I should be extraordinarily angry if this happened to me, unless the thing came from Woolworths, then I would take it for the joke it is. The only piece of jewellery I ever owned was my engagement ring, which I lost shortly after my marriage. I never made any attempt to trace it. It would be awful to me to think I had to keep a precious part of my mind engaged in wondering if bits of coloured glass were 'safe'. But this must not be a universal thought, or the jeweller — and many of the police — would perish. We have a whole house that can be left unprotected at night simply because there is nothing in it worth taking away. Nobody in their senses would take our chairs and beds and books. I don't collect rare books or autographs, or indeed, anything but flesh; and death will come for that in his good time.

To get back to our visitor. He's a born giver, and has an elusive face. That is, I can never remember what he is like when he is not here. I do know that most people either like or dislike him intensely, but I hope I hover judiciously outside the radius of his personality. The other day, he left his hat. Even his hat reeks of personality, but that day it reeked of mothballs — a smell I hate above all others.

I asked him afterwards why his hat smelled of mothballs, and he said it was because it had to. He had stopped his car to give a shilling to an old tramp, because he suddenly felt that he must, and the surprised tramp had plunged a hand into the bottom of the sack he carried and given our friend a handful of mothballs. There was nowhere to put them but in his hat. I love any story of two lives momentarily touching.

We played darts, and he won all the time. The more he won, the odder were the ways in which he played, throwing the darts three at a time, or back to front, or turned round himself away from the board, or throwing them under his legs. He does not at all mind telling stories against himself. At the seaside, one wet day, he had taken a boatful of children fishing. At the end of an hour, only three fish had been caught, and the children were behaving like fiends, so he got the fisherman to trawl across the bay, and in this way, the boat was soon filled with fish. Pandemonium broke out, for two minutes after the plenty had arrived, the little ones were all fighting between themselves for the biggest fish. He is always getting himself into scenes like this, taking out carloads of children, and buying them ice-cream. How strange it is that one can only know the outside of a life like this, and never the in. He always reminds me of somebody mortally wounded, and yet singing and dancing and laughing. I don't know why.

But one of the reasons I like him, I find, is that he noticed our oasis of work in this desert of garden. Already it looks as if it has been this way since the beginning of time. And next year, when the flowers come up — will you notice how space and time has gone by the board? Next year, when the flowers come up, it should be a thing of beauty. I can already see crocuses and snowdrops, though not a bulb has been bought yet; and tulips in the sheltered place, under the windows, so that the strong winds shall not beat them down.

When the man had gone, my husband and I sat up talking about meteorites, wondering what would happen if one landed in a crowded part of England. What a marvellous death — biff! It is surprising how much can be found to say about meteorites. Before we went to bed, we had already disposed of the world, splitting it up into fragments, which whirled about for ever in space. However, I can face the prospect with equanimity.

Nicholas and his cousin Donald (still whooping) are having a friendly fight with sticks of rhubarb picked from a patch in what is left of the kitchen garden, which have their huge leaves still on them. I need only turn my head to see them doing something new. They are inventive children, and have simply to see a thing like a sack of cement and a watering can to produce surprising and unexpected and sometimes costly results. Costly to remove, I mean.

The wireless is off love and on string quartets today. I always seem to hear the space *between* the strings in quartets, and the sound there is very melancholy. Some days I am alive to music and thankful for it, and others, nothing can comfort me like silence. I have loved three films for different reasons: *Green Pastures*, *Scarface*, and an older one, *King of Jazz*. In the last one was a scene where a gigantic negro, or his shadow, jumped upon a drum, so far as I can remember. No sound was heard but a rhythmic thump, very satisfying. I feel that everything is going with a rhythmic thump just now, in armaments factories and marriage beds alike, so all should be for the best in this best of possible worlds. But I am forgetting my quest for truth, and God is as far from me as ever.

13

This hilltop lost its beauty many, many years ago. Almost the only trees upon it are the eastward-bending ones in this garden. There are abandoned stone quarries within a stone's throw of the house which have a grim and murderous beauty — now and then they lure somebody to a quick doom — and bare fields covered with coarse grass; and new houses. But there is a wide sky, and a fresh sweet wind always blowing.

Perhaps the people about here are no kinder than they are anywhere else, but they seem so. I have known many of them all my life. When my brother fell ill at the age of twenty-two of a mixture of consumption and unrequited love, the neighbours were always coming round with some little tempting delicacy for him. If one cooked a chicken, the best was brought for him, and every baking day some cake or other was carried in careful and often workworn hands. I suppose these people knew he was going to die, but we didn't. There had always been the eleven of us. But their unfailing kindness made my mother weep, and she did not cry easily.

And when my brother died, and the long, light coffin was taken from the house, I only remember that there was a plate on it, which read 'In his twenty-third year', and it seemed to me then, and still seems one of the saddest sentences I had ever read.

A friend accuses me of being a provincial, as if this were a thing to be ashamed of. If being a provincial means loving with an unreasoning love a small patch of this earth which I have always known, and being glad I was born on it, and hoping I shall die there, then I am a provincial.

I like London, but to have to live there for ever would be exile indeed. I came back from London on Friday, and now it is Sunday night. Many and deep seas of time lie between Friday and Sunday.

The man from the BBC fed me beautifully, but he did not tell me any funny stories, as so many people in London do. It is quite possible that not one of the few I know would amuse him. He is a very serious man, and I believe he expected to find me much more serious than I am.

Our meeting took place at his club. He had said that he might be late, but I love waiting, so I was there on time. People often say it is impossible to keep an appointment in London. I don't think so. You have simply to allow for traffic delays, which always happen. Business is different. I have been used to business men all my life, and by now I know that the rush comes at the last minute because the whole day before it has been spent in a kind of delicious dawdling which is called 'reviewing the situation'. That last minute rush is the spice of life for the business man, and also his secretary, who then has a genuine grievance, a real something to live for in a world of make-believe.

The doorman in that manly place looked at me with a face of resigned suffering, and gave me explicit instructions about the Ladies' Room, which I did not want or need. He then turned to a newcomer, leaving me mentally stranded in this unwanted boudoir. I waited till he had finished, and then said 'And what next?' He intimated a drawing-room. In a dream-like way, I followed his instructions, so that I really landed in the Ladies' Room, and for lack of something else to do, got myself a glass of water with hands that trembled.

I love meeting new people, one at a time, and I am

no longer shy. But once, I was very shy indeed, and at intervals an agonizing shadow of stage-fright comes over me still when I am to meet someone quite new. Even my hands grow cold and clammy. But I have found a cure for that. I say to myself, 'Never give anybody a hand like a wet cod. You know how you hate receiving them'. And I concentrate on getting my hands warm by folding them over my arms, underneath my sleeves. This is a very calming effort in itself, and usually successful.

Friends warned me that I should be meeting a very charming man, if he were from the BBC, but fortunately this proved to be untrue. I loathe charming men. They are the only creatures who reduce me to silence. I do remember his first speech, which took place on the stairs going down to the dining-room, and which was, 'So the children didn't get mumps, after all?' and we were launched upon a sea of words and sank in it like the ship which was launched and sank to the bottom of the harbour, and we didn't come up again until everybody else had finished and gone. He said we would have coffee upstairs, and then grinned and said, 'Let's have it where we are.' This seemed a sensible suggestion, so we stayed where we were, and after that talked ourselves into the Mall, and across roads and past people until we found ourselves in Bond Street, where we parted with sudden violence.

I know nothing whatever about this man except that we are both looking for God and the truth, and that we have not made much headway. Usually observant, I cannot remember his appearance or whether he was tall or short, but I liked what we said. Perhaps this was simply a meeting of two people who were shy inside but not out. If that is so, it will have to remain a kind of grim secret between him and me, for I am certain nobody else would believe it of either of us.

And this only brings me angrily to the fact that I have spent the last half-hour brushing my husband's suit with ammonia and water, exactly as I did in the old days. He goes off to London tomorrow morning, and all the clothes he has are hanging dirtily and drunkenly in his wardrobe, covered with gardening stains. And my household is denuded of all its help. I have been too generous with my holidays-with-pay, inducing homesickness. Fan and Delia wanted to leave. I am very human and easily touched, and I don't want to have anybody in my house who is pining to be somewhere else, so after my first feeling of dismay had subsided — I *did* want some tea — my spirits rose, and I said, 'Do you want to work out your notice, or would you rather have your money and go home today?' They looked at each other, and voted for home, so everything was nicely arranged yesterday, and here I am today as I was a month ago.

How I love change, really! It seems impossible that Fan and Delia have been with me for eighteen months. Nicholas is six and a half, and baby two and a quarter, and if it were not for my increasing longing to adopt still another child, we could be a quiet and sedate family, ambling steadily along in the house with a little outside help for the rough work — work which I can do best of all, but of which I know I should soon tire.

So tomorrow, Mrs Fitzpatrick, who has been appearing at odd crises for the last few years, will come in to help. But like me and the BBC man, she can talk — though she can talk and work. If she has to be in a room alone, there is a kind of depressed silence hanging about the house. If I catch her accidentally being silent, it seems to me that her face is filled with actual suffering. But baby loves her passionately, and now that baby can talk, she and Mrs Fitzpatrick can entertain each other conversationally for hours.

For three days, London was marvellous. But I had taken two pairs of tight shoes, and so the place became black with horror. On the Tuesday night, I bought myself a pair of black slippers, and went out to dinner defiantly wearing them, and then on to the Holborn Empire. I soon forgot my feet and enjoyed all the time-worn jokes, remembering nothing of the programme but one sentence, which reminded me vaguely of the late Frank Harris, 'Love's like everything else. You have to begin at the bottom.'

14

Because my husband is away, I am having my meals when and how I like — this is not a joke — and yet wondering why it is that women run so to eggs. I have just poached the perfect specimen, and had it on brown toast, with China tea as an accompaniment at the strange hour of six-twenty.

I have bathed baby and put her to bed. Nicholas is out visiting. He promised to be home at half-past six, but that means seven, as he is sure to find something of absorbing interest in the two hundred yards of ground he has to cover. The wireless, in perfect accord with my mood, is giving gramophone records of operatic selections. Somehow they match the poached egg — the Prologue to *Pagliacci*, and 'Even bravest hearts may swell', from Gounod's *Faust*. I like these two, because I know every note and its shadow, and have known them almost all my life.

In my early youth, I began to love opera with a love which has weakened but never died. I think it was the gorgeous row the singers made which enslaved me. 'Yah, yah, yah, yah', they still yell in gorgeous abandon. The death songs pierced my heart where a scene from a play left it cold. I did everything but steal money so that I could get a seat in the gallery of the Theatre Royal when a rare Opera Company came to the town. I drowned voluptuously in the easy music as one might in a butt of Malmsey wine.

Twice I have heard Turner's Opera Company perform. They were a gallant troupe. I do not know what has now happened to these people, but I will swear that every aged but indomitable member of that wonderful band will go to some unique operatic heaven, and God will make town after town for them to trek to, and he will provide them with a loving and enthusiastic audience, of whom I hope I may make one. I can see again those great sparkling eyes, that heavy paint which only deepened the wrinkles of age, the terrific blueness which shone through the make-up; and I can hear again that passion and sincerity which is the only excuse for performance.

I have just finished reading Freda Strindberg's *Marriage With Genius*, after enjoying every word of it. 'Enjoying' seems ghoulish, as if one should get pleasure from a film of a fight to the death. How can we, how dare we try to present another person, when it is an impossibility even to present ourselves? Even by means of letters, for, Lord, what letters we can write when we want to do that! There is a good deal of space lying between our eyes and a sheet of writing paper, and things seem to alter between the head and the hand. I wonder how much and how often Strindberg meant this — or if at all: 'I do not know, but it seems to me as though the past alone were bearable, the living moment is always doleful.'

It is true, though. The living moment, when we concentrate on it, is always doleful, and Strindberg must have concentrated on it with grim intensity all the time. Dissect one fragment of time, and where are you?

Where am I? Here is my adopted son, reading the evening paper, one knee up and one knee down, his fair hair darkened on this side which is away from the light of evening. He has twisted round and shown me a hole in the seat of his trousers with an expression of great surprise. It is the first of what I suppose will be many. Baby is by now fast asleep in her cot. My husband is in London. So I suppose I should look at the living moment and find it doleful, but I don't want to. There is a fire, and that is such good company.

Reading of Strindberg has reminded me of staying in Paris. We often make great mistakes about hotels, in our attempts to find the happy medium, that cross between a palace and a knocking shop. And we are always willing to take the advice of people we meet in trains, though it has led us to some funny places.

It was just after I had started to write myself that somebody told us of an hotel 'on the left bank' which was *really* French, though quantities of English writers stayed there. We had only one night, the room was red and full of mosquitoes, and the proprietress had the meanest face I ever saw on a woman, the food was bad and dear, and I did not like being near the river. Those living moments were doleful enough.

But the very next day we met an American dance-band drummer on another train, and full of hope and faith, we went to stay at the hotel he had just left. It was up in Montmartre and was really cheap. There was a divan bed, and large windows, and up one step, so that you didn't have to move out of the room, was a complete bathroom, hidden by a night-blue curtain. Everything was blue, the carpet, the bedspread, the easy chairs. In our casual way, we have lost it, but some day it may return to us, just as may the restaurant where I had a perfect Chateaubriand steak. Why do things go down into some well of memory? That place holds blue divans, steaks, and American dance-band drummers, throwing them up to me today for no known reason. I hope some of the drummer's dreams have come true, for he was a very ambitious man, and may, for all I know, now own some celebrated name which is even printed on gramophone records.

After a year or so of sensible living, I find myself downstairs at three o'clock in the morning, drinking hot milk, listening to records on the radiogram, and having insomnia, which I never get unless I have something very exciting to think about. Soon, I shall listen in to some distant station, if the gradually soothed feeling which hot milk gives me does not come into its own.

If I had spent the night in a house filled with strangers — though what is my house, or any house, but that? — I should have lain wakeful, staring into the blackness of a particularly dark night, with my mind off pitch. For tonight, I have been a little shaken by the events of the day, and my brain cannot settle down to its usual pace, but is racketing. The children are admirable sleepers; even if they were not, they would have to get used to the idea that they own a mother who likes to keep odd hours and listen to odd music.

Perhaps it is not true that we are so much alone as we think. I believe I have made a faint contact with another mind, and this revelation has torn me from a not-so-comfortable sleep, and sent me downstairs for milk and music. Yet the whole thought is disturbing. I don't want to have an influence on anybody. And when somebody suddenly sees a mildly-stated point of view, and after fighting and struggling, turns, and decides to take it, the shadow of 'influence' falls. Perhaps something will happen tomorrow which will show me that I am wrong. I started out to sleep with an unsolved problem in my head, and while I slept, the pieces sorted themselves and waked me to violent knowledge. It also gives me a new slant on myself.

Yes, in this silent night, I will say that mind can

reach mind, however I retract tomorrow. For being a woman, I had thought that the mind could only be reached through the body. I believe I was secretly cynical about it, having proved the idea to my satisfaction. I have been wrong. I must be wrong, or how could people live with any pleasure between middle age and old age?

I have a growing desire to hear what America is howling into the silent night. Are we all inane? Are there unplumbed depths, and is it worth while to dive into them now and again, if only to get the feeling of space? Night is good, and wisdom is to be sought in it. There is a mental clarity, a falling away of dross for a little while; a feeling of deeper humility and greater gratitude than have gone before; a kind of growing-pain.

This calls for a long walk over the downs in the moonlight. But there are no downs here, and no moonlight. Only two children to be protected and remembered.

The world must be full of women who sit at home making old pillowslips into instruments of torture by unpicking the ends, cutting the middles, and sewing the result into an abhorrent lump across the centre. Far sooner would I sleep with my head on clean, soft rag than on that inspired boulder. I have just been reading a magazine packed with hints from people who are holding civilization back by centuries.

Can *this* be possible? '*Something to Make*. Get a small flowerpot and paint the outside with some black paint. Gum a piece of felt on bottom of pot to prevent scratching the table, etc. Place a small piece of cardboard inside pot to stop the sand from coming out of the bottom. Arrange two sprays of artificial flowers and fill up with sand or mould. Sprinkle top with artificial moss.'

But why? Why? And if one, why not two, four, a hundred? What is to stop anyone from filling the world with these monstrosities? Because that does happen. It makes me want to start a home magazine, What *Not* to Do, Don't Make an Ornamental Flowerpot, Let your old Blankets Decay in Peace, Burn your Cauliflower Stalks instead of trying to make French Soup out of them.

But who am I to advise? I am not the perfect house-wife. Not many people would like a household like ours. There is never a needle to be found here, so of course, buttons fall off and stay off. But nobody nags about it. I have found that such trivialities don't really matter. One gradually learns to acquire garments without buttons. And kind-hearted visitors, who travel about with sewing compendiums in large bags, come every now and again, and sew the most necessary buttons on for us. I commend them in such a heartfelt way that their labour becomes a pleasure. I also let them know carelessly that if they didn't do it, some-body else would. So there is perpetual competition for our mending.

Of course, not all days are good. There are mornings filled with a kind of despair, and afternoons of sunless gloom, when the children quarrel senselessly, and keep coming to me with complaints, and I am no Solomon. Though only the two of them live here, another two, nephew and niece, of the same ages, spend most of their waking hours with us. Today, the position is reversed, and my children have gone to spend the day with their cousins in the village. I must admit that I am filled with delight because I am alone for a while.

For a whole week, I have never been out of the house, except across the fields to the bus to meet the hairdresser. Firelighting, pleasant as it is, makes hair sooty, and I do not want to be a dirty woman. This girl is very pretty, and it is a pleasure to have her in the house. It must be nice to be tall, and young, and fair, and to have a certain amount of robust commonsense.

I wonder if the young ones of today are really more sensible than we used to be. It appears so. And they also look nicer, too — or is that merely my imagination? There was too much 'frip' in the Edwardian days — all right, this, for people with plenty of money for changes, but not so good for the near-poor, who looked bedraggled too early and too often. There seems to be a happy medium now between the frivolous things and the sensible ones. We look good in showers today, where rain used to be all enemy.

A plague of colds-in-the-head has descended on us with the turn of the weather. But it is the first we have had this year, and it is already autumn. The trees are thinning, and the sun hangs lower in the sky. I feel angry to think that I was born in September, and so missed a summer. If I have one grudge against my parents, it is this. I am never quite warm enough, except in the Turkish baths.

My birthday is on the first official day of autumn, and I am looking forward to it. Because, after all, forty-two is forty-two, and there's nothing to do but be hearty about it. It is certainly better (to me) than being half that, because my twenty-first birthday fell in the middle of the war, the horror of which never leaves me. I seemed to be, like everybody else, completely at the mercy of elements outside my control.

I cannot think of any 'best time' in my life — or, if I can, I shall not dilate upon it. But I early realized the delightful irresponsibility of first childhood, which Nicholas seems to possess, too, in full measure. It might be unfortunate that I haven't let it all go, even at this age. A tremendous bill arrived, surprising even my husband, this morning. When he protested, I said to him in astonishment, 'But I've had all these things. I wanted them, I took the trouble to choose them, and now I'm enjoying them with all my heart. You have only to pay for them.'

I think God ought to be pleased once a week if he hears the people singing to a cinema organ's accompaniment 'All the nice girls love a sailor', and 'I do like to be beside the seaside, I do like to be beside the sea!' This generally happens on a Saturday, and I hear it in a kind of ecstatic peace, because my husband takes the children out to tea, and I have the afternoon to myself. On Saturdays, I don't want to hear the finest string quartets in the world. I want nothing but Harold Ramsay at the organ of the Union Cinema, Kingston-on-Thames. There's nothing whiny about Harold. He can make everybody sing. And it sounds like a paean of thanksgiving.

I am beginning to wonder if I am too easily satisfied — too grateful, and too easygoing. Now and then, I am hauled fiercely over red-hot coals by somebody who tells me that I give too much away to some persons and not enough to others. The ones who tell me are invariably of the 'other' party. They don't really tell me. They point it out, or show me in some way how unnecessary it is to do anything for so-and-so, who is quite able to fend for himself, but the people who just bear things with a bright smile, and never complain, *they* are the ones who really need help.

This sort of talk depresses me. The best part of the joy of giving — which is a form of depravity — is the fierce joy of giving where you want to do it, not being forced into contemplation of the world's bright smilers and silent sufferers. I never suffer silently myself. I yell when there is anything to yell about, because that seems right and natural to me. And when I am better, I yell with joy, and advertise that fact, too.

Last night, the doctor called about six o'clock, which is a time he has never chosen before. But it was his birthday, and he knew we had a present for him, and he had come for it — a pair of winter gloves. It was baking day, and I had the loaves in their tins on the hearth in front of a hot fire, and the guard was up. I had asked the children if they would like to be bathed on the hearthrug, and they had enthusiastically said yes.

Baby was just finished, and she looked clean and beautiful in her long, white nightdress. Her eyes are singularly large and trusting, and I think she will be beautiful when she grows up, though her generous mouth is slightly out of proportion now. And Nick was sitting in fresh hot water, washing himself very soapily when the doctor came. We were all so much surprised that we forgot to wish him many happy returns.

He is a very sensible man, with children of his own, so he nursed baby whilst I dried Nick and put his pyjamas on, and then he took away the bath and emptied the water down the kitchen sink, and came back and said, 'Why, the house is much cleaner and tidier without any maids in it.' Perhaps I have earned this compliment. But he came in at a lucky moment, when our hearts were filled with peace and love and tiredness. Anyhow, it was a change from the pain and suffering of which he will see so much.

My mind keeps going back to the bread. I am glad it is especially nice this week, baked light and crisp and golden-brown. There is no doubt that it is a pleasure to have a husband who is at any rate a temporary capitalist, because money does some of the loveliest things that can be done in this life. Perhaps I am fortunate in not wanting the things that are spoken of as pleasures in this world. I don't want a lot of clothes, and I don't want to be seen in expensive places. I would certainly like to go to theatres more, but somehow there is never time; when I am in London, there are too many people and too much talk; and in this town, if there is a good play, it is always put on when I cannot possibly see it. Perhaps I was a scene shifter in a former life, and am now being given a rest from the stage. But there are pleasures to look forward to, for ever. I have never tried fishing, or golf, or bridge, or even tennis or riding a bicycle or crocheting doilys.

15

Winter is over and gone, and the voice of the turtle is heard in the land. When did we learn to call time by name? Seven months have passed, and made very little difference to my spirit; there would be thick places and thin places in it, but I have happily forgotten them.

My father has died, so now I am an old orphan. But death in age is a natural thing. I have never cared for anybody so much that I desire their perpetual company. Now that both my parents are dead, I must say that I think of my mother with the kind of comic tenderness I feel for myself, because we saw through each other, and yet liked each other as human beings. She had a much purer mind than I have, and a nicer nature. She would help people in an unobtrusive way, whereas I do it gruffly and gauchely, though I mean well.

Yes, my father was alive, and he is now dead. Towards the end, he travelled back through life, and died thinking he was a young man in the pride of his strength. His hands — I lifted them on to the coverlet when he wanted to change his position — were like a turkey's claws, yellow and hard, with bony arms at the end of them. He tried to put them beneath the bedclothes after a little while, and couldn't, so I put them back. My only other memories of him, through a lifetime, are of dutifully raising my cheek for his kiss, and feeling the texture of his beard on my skin. And of his looking up from a book — he always sat in the parlour — when we grew too noisy in our childish play, and saying in a wheedling voice, 'Run to your mamma, now.' We ran.

What should a woman feel towards her male parent? There is so much written about natural love between fathers and daughters. I can imagine great and unbreakable bonds between husbands and wives who live in amity, who talk together and have many of the same interests and one or two different ones. But it must be rare and wonderful to have a loved father. I don't remember that my father ever deviated from his set course, or gave up anything, or exerted himself in any way for the good of humanity. Neither do I see why he should have done so if he didn't want to. But he got the consequences of his behaviour — and bore them with the same indifference.

We went for the Easter holidays to Greystoke, a little village in Cumberland. My sister-in-law's father is the village carpenter there, and at Easter he was busy making a coffin for a child who had died. We went into the churchyard at Dacre the day after the funeral, and there, I saw the place where I would like to be buried.

Dacre has a beautiful church, but it is the churchyard that I love. In it are four stone figures, supposed to be dancing bears. They are very ancient. Two of them look like lions to me — the lions in the court of the Alhambra — the third one is grief personified, and the fourth inexplicable. But the clouds and sunshine of April I want to have over my bones. How quickly bones and stones crumble.

I am one of the few remaining people who think that time is orderly, and that it goes right on and not backwards and forwards. It is only when you stop to

119

think about it that queer things happen. But it doesn't stop the blossom from fruiting or the seed from sprouting.

Now that the young part of my life is over, with its struggle and strife, and I am beginning to be bodily comfortable, I think perhaps I wouldn't mind a year or two of the past back, if I could pick my years. Life has been like a rather exciting party, which went off well in patches, but I am tired now, the particularly charming guests have gone, and I am thinking of my narrow bed with more joy than sorrow.

The holiday in Cumberland was good, and I climbed Carrick fell in new shoes. A month before that, I had had the bones of my toes straightened, so it was not bad going. This is a very little fell, and an accommodating one. There is something of challenge in every hill, and this was no exception. My brother went with me. The hill won, for we did not reach the top. It was nearly one o'clock, and we were keeping the rest of the family waiting. So we turned back. We were so near the summit that the slope was almost perpendicular. We were climbing in a spread-eagled way, and the slippery grass began to betray us. We turned back.

As we slipped thankfully downwards, we could see the pigmy figures of the others on the white road below. The air was cool and sweet, the ground very dry beneath our feet. Now and again, a few loose stones rattled from under our shoes, and though we were descending quickly, our consciences made it seem slow. Then suddenly we stopped and laughed. What was the use of this polite lying and hurrying? The others would wait on our caprice for hours, if necessary. Why hadn't they made the climb? Probably because they thought it was a waste of effort. Why had we tried and failed? We didn't know that, either; but we got a kindly welcome.

Twice we had tea in a tiny pub isolated on a moor. The old landlady came in to talk to us. She had had five other strangers in for tea over Easter, and was thrilled by that contact with the great world. We noticed that the sugar had lowered in the basin between Sunday and Tuesday — she took it out of a cupboard in a corner of the room — and that was how we learned of the other people.

She brought in a volume of a history of Cumberland for me to see, as we had visited the grounds of a large castle at the weekend, and my mind had been disturbed more than a little. It was such an elaborate place, and so tasteless except where Nature had been given a hand. And so expensive, so crammed with unnecessary ornaments from another country that it filled me with rage. The day before that, we had driven through an idle colliery town, where the grey paint was peeling from the grey walls, and where even the children's voices — if there were any — seemed stilled by a palpable heaviness in the whole atmosphere. So far as I could learn from the history of Cumberland, this colliery town and the property beneath it — even to the land under the sea — was owned by the very people who had caused shiploads of expensive junk to be tipped in their gardens. There seemed a disproportion in the whole thing, too big for me to do anything but grieve about.

The quiet country people took my outburst, when it came, very quietly. They said that the gentry — their name for the people who had lived for generations in large houses and castles — had always been the gentry and always would be, and that, anyway, they liked to curtsy to them and to work for them. Back I went to the history of Cumberland. I wanted to see what king had decorated this particular earl and for what bravery, but all I found was that in the seventeenth century a simple Missus, even as you or I, had 'bought the lordship for three thousand pounds'. My next research in history will be to find where she got her three thousand pounds.

The relations of my sister-in-law didn't believe it. They had seen the gentry being the gentry all their lives, and they knew that everything that was printed wasn't necessarily true. They don't differentiate between a newspaper and an authentic history of Cumberland.

How complacently one accepts, on holiday! Here are these great hills — for me. Here is this sky — for me. Here is this farmhouse, these beautifully cooked and well-planned meals — for me. I have the habit of letting a new place shoot itself into me in one piece. Then it is always there. It happens in a flash, without effort. I have been with people who must sit and gaze at scenery for hours, and then take a map and put names to all the lovely places. I have only to shut my eyes and see again any place I wish to see, in all its detail. The further I go into my childhood, the more distinct it becomes. The red glow in the northern sky from the fire lighted on the top of Wrose Hill for Queen Victoria's Diamond Jubilee is an indelible picture.

Life has gone too smoothly and slothfully the last seven months. There must have been incidents of all kinds — the children have grown, and in their growing might have spilled pearls of wisdom which I have forgotten to string.

We have a friend who writes her children's sayings in a little book. I have never seen this book, but the odd bits she has told me are genuinely funny. My children aren't funny. Nicholas uses long words, but he uses them appropriately, and they don't sound odd to me if they do to other people. But in times of illness and frailness, he has come out with Paul Dombey-like sentences, suddenly, such as 'When I am in Heaven —' which have temporarily terrified me. And baby Jane persists in saying 'Don't go out with me', when she means the exact opposite. Otherwise they remain normal.

Wars are still drearily going on. There has been a long period of drought, and the newspapers have foretold the failure of crops. They also do this when there is a flood, which seems to happen whenever there is no drought.

And people have written still more books about the mystery of the plays and sonnets of Shakespeare. It would be a pleasant change for someone to write of the still deeper mystery that lies behind the production of these books. Why must we give ourselves this eternal appearance of occupation? Looked at in a moment's rest, we seem like a world of ants. No, we must go on shoving things about, produce food, and children, and guns to shoot each other with. We don't want to do it, but we do it. No wonder there are dictators. One man with a little more energy than the rest of us can pull a million. He uses the force in others for his own ends. *They* make the image, not the man himself. But presently he must see himself as a god; poor creature.

During the winter, I went to see my first film labelled 'For Adults Only'. As I went in during the course of it, and came out before it had connected up, because I was with a restless friend who said it was 'too slow', I shall never be quite sure what it was all about. It featured a tragic-eyed woman who swam part of the time, leaving her clothes on her horse, or rather her mare. This mare was feeling ruttish, and sprinted away when she heard a trumpeting stallion. The rest of the film showed the same thing happening to the woman, but more slowly and less naturally. The stallion in this case was a lover with a magnificent torso, but on the other hand, her husband wore pince-nez. I think adultery is committed because people need a change now and again. Monogamy is a state, and not a virtue.

Nicholas has gone to Morecambe with Peg. Peg was plucked from the pages of the *Daily Telegraph*. Seven months ago, I advertised there for a new housekeeper, and got Peg. They do exist, scattered about the hemisphere like diamonds, nice and pleasant girls who will come to a house like this and work — quietly, passionately and uncomplainingly — even happily, for twenty-five shillings a week, a half-day and an evening, and one weekend a month. The first words she said when I took her upstairs on her arrival were, 'Oh, what a lovely room'. And she smiled.

We had got the room looking rather nice. It had white walls and pale green paint. There was a divan bed, and an easy chair covered in green and white, with curtains to match them. There was a wireless, and a row of books in a rack, and a gas fire. And somebody had sent her a sheaf of pale pink roses.

Peg is of Scotch descent, and knows when to open her mouth and when to keep it shut, which is something I have never learned. She is twenty-five years old, and those twenty-five years, except for a few photographs and fewer words, are a closed book to me. But the last seven months are not. I admire and respect Peg. She is conscientious, a state-of-being which rarely comes my way. I collect the happy-go-lucky around me, the rollicking roarers, the 'never mind, there's plenty more where that came from' kind. Peg can keep people in their places — and this means me. She pins me down to yes or no, instead of letting me leave things in a fluid state.

So I let the seven months flow over my head, as if I had been drowned in a river of bliss, but now I shall have to wake from it, for Peg has gone and got herself engaged, and will be married in September. I am glad for her, but sorry for myself. She will bake those lemon pies for her husband, and not for mine. She will dash neatly and efficiently about, and spend the right amount of pennies in the right kind of shop. Her fiancé comes to see her now and then.

The younger girl who replaces Delia is nearly too handsome to live, and she has a way with men. It is such a devastating way that the tradesmen have gone down before her like a row of ninepins, and we are getting flawless fruit, vegetables, fish, and meat. She once came to help for a short time when she was sixteen, and in the chrysalis state. Now she is eighteen, as beautiful as a butterfly, but not as proud as a queen. Her hair is fair, and she has had it dyed to a shade she calls honey-coloured. She curls it with curling-tongs. Her skin is very white, but she tints her cheeks to a pinkish glow. Her lips are pale, so she makes them scarlet. Her eyelashes and brows are golden, and she blackens them. She is five feet ten inches tall, and still growing. When she is dressed to go out, she looks like — well, I hesitate to say — anyhow, she looks lovely, and I often wish she were in suitable hands. Something could be made out of her. And I don't know what. I try to waken her mind to good books. She takes to them prettily, and sometimes even reads them, and mentions them afterwards. But she can roll a languishing eye, and would rather read, I am afraid, a cloudy-looking bluish journal called *My Weekly*.

When I see this tall, golden creature coming into my room with a tray, I am filled with perpetual astonishment. The hand that has so expertly pulled a beer-pump, and elegantly touched that headful of rolled curls with manicured fingers can wash up the dishes just as purposefully four times a day, and blacklead the grate on Fridays. She laughs at me, and says I am a 'one'; and she likes me.

This lovely being had been here five months before I noticed that Peg did not always see eye to eye with her. There were subterranean rumbles in the house. Anne was temperamental. There were days when she loved to work, and days when she just wouldn't. And the work was not being properly divided. But then, neither were the wages, for Anne only gets fourteen shillings to Peg's twenty-five. What was to be done?

Change is the solution to everything, so I have sent Peg to Morecambe for a short holiday with Nicholas, and there she is at present, until I can solve the problem of Anne. I told them they could both go home for the Easter holiday, but they preferred to stay. Peg's fiancé came over, but Anne's young man of the moment didn't, so she was able to put on a terrific display of temperament because the family was away, and things have never been the same in the kitchen since.

I had word from Peg this morning, thanking me for the registered letter. I packed her off with Nick in such a hurry on Wednesday morning that there was no time to give them much money. She says:

'We have a front sitting-room and the bedroom

126

above.

'Nick seems very happy and is very much at home. At present he is out playing with the little girl who lives here. We are out usually from nine-thirty a.m. to twelve forty-five p.m. and from two p.m. to four forty-five p.m. Nicholas, with his hired tricycle, a beautiful maroon one, almost new, and spade and pail, and I go off each time to the beach beside the old harbour wall.

'Nicholas wants me to say he got his pocket-money, and thanks you very much. Also, can he stay till Whitsuntide? The reason for this is that he is very disappointed that the merry-go-rounds, etc., do not begin until then. The tricycle comes out to eleven-pence halfpenny per day for hire. I hope I have not been too extravagant with this. Considering the joy it gives, it is worth it. The hire expires on Wednesday night. Shall I renew it?

'I don't think there is anything more at present.'

I call that a nice letter. There is much more in it, of a private nature. And there is a neat scrap of paper with every item of expenditure on it. Even 'Ice-cream, 2d.'

Here comes Anne with my tea. We have got a folding tray-table, and it is as useful as even the advertisement says. She unfolds it, and puts it down near me. She is wearing a purple dress with a tiny apron that she has made herself, and I tell her once more that she looks beautiful, and she tells me once more that I am a 'one'.

This spring is, of course, one of the memories that the modern young should take down the ages with them, as my generation take the summers of nineteen eleven and nineteen twenty-one. There is sunshine every morning. Wild birds keep on singing regardless of the ginger farmyard cat. It is almost too lovely, the freshness of this renewal.

Baby — Jane, now she is nearly three — came in and said she had bromide on toast for breakfast. I have made no further inquiries; this seems good enough for me. And we went to see an English film last night — the kind that makes the English feel hot and ashamed. They hope no foreigner will ever see it. Hundreds of feet of riotous and undisciplined fun to begin with, and with it, laughter which raises a sense of gratitude. Then, somewhere, sheer bleakness sets in. The situations repeat themselves, laughter dies. The point comes where in an old music-hall, the audience would have risen and silently tramped out, one behind the other, without raising eyes to the stage. But we are trained to a passive indifference. A good film surprises us. We bear the bad ones.

But perhaps all acting is just being alive. When we wake in the morning, we arrange our parts for the day. The funny part is that we don't know the play — whether it will turn out to be tragic, or comic, or merely boring. And we may no longer be there by night. It is odd to speculate on where we might be, but not — to me — fruitful. I don't know. I met an ardent spiritualist two years ago. He had no doubts whatever about the matter of the survival of each particular spirit after death. And he would listen to no criticism of his theories. If anybody made a humorous remark (and many tried) he squashed them with his scorn. 'Why should you try to query, by your sniggers, my reseach of twenty-five years?' And if you say, 'But what is the result of your research?' he will answer, 'Read my books'.

I have never doubted his sincerity, never given the ghost of a laugh at his trembling earnestness, but I cannot read his books — they don't make sense to me. Nor can I really care whether I survive after death or not. It must be a burning question, but what is behind it? If you are not there, somebody very much like you will fill the niche, as a new man is got for the job when the old man dies. What *is* this desire for survival? If you were in the utmost bodiless bliss, could you ever forget the sorrows, the senseless cruelties of this world? Could you understand them — or forgive them?

Now I am remembering something which doesn't apply here, but it may fall back into the well if I don't take it out and dry it. I chanced an odd eye in the Tube to read a few lines of a manuscript somebody was reading from: 'and as Noel Coward says in his epic *Cavalcade*, "What shall it profit a man if he gain the whole world and lose his own soul".'

Of course, we must know we are crazy, and in a crazy world. But was it ever anything else? Would any man own up to being wicked, to loving evil, unless he wanted to boast or make an impression on minds weaker than his own. And how soon illness could flatten *him* out — even the pain of toothache, or if he had no teeth, earache. Examine any newspaper. On the one hand, provocative articles are written in them. On the other, readers say mildly, 'Look at this nonsense'. Too often, a wild journalistic outburst is followed by the meekest of apologies. But we all know what hair-tearings, what shoutings and revilings, what boot-lickings, what storms in an egg-cup have gone into that apology, that is, if we follow our films at all well.

One newspaper has given me much tender delight. There is a review in it of my last lot of stories called 'Ravensthorpe Woman's Fourth Book'. It cannot possibly give anybody the pleasure it gives me, but it illustrates a point.

'Yorkshire authors generally have been exceedingly active during the last few months, and foremost among them is a former Ravensthorpe woman — Mrs Malachi Whitaker — whose fourth book of stories has this week been published. This gifted writer, who now lives in Hull Road, Hornsea, first received an elementary education, afterwards passing on to Dudley Training College, where she studied to become a school teacher. When quite young she brought out her first two books, which dealt with religious topics, and were put into words which children of seven could easily understand.

'With the reception this was given, Mrs Whitaker produced her second book, *Children and How to Deal with Them*, and, incidentally, the author has no children of her own.

'Her latest achievement, however, is her best, and as one London critic puts it, "She has Tchekov, Poe, Kipling, Bret Harte, and O. Henry all beaten into a frazzle".'

Alas! I don't know where Ravensthorpe is, I don't live in Hull Road, Hornsea, I never passed on to Dudley Training College, and never wrote those delicious books on religious topics or *Children and How to Deal with Them*. I don't know how to deal with them. Nor have I ever beaten anybody into a frazzle. But this is just a mild sample of what a newspaper can do.

We sat up too late last night. As we watched the film, one of Anne's particular young men came to see her, and we entered the house at half-past ten to find her bemusedly kneading dough for bread. She said, Well, she had forgotten it. Bread must be given its head — an hour to rise, an hour in the tins, and three-quarters or thereabouts in the oven. Anne saw no earthly reason why she should not stay up until half-past one. I had to give a direct order for once, 'Go to bed'. And she was so astonished that she went.

17

We have taken a flat at the seaside for the summer, so that now we look over a long stretch of pebbles and sand to the hills of Cumberland. The three-balled lights on the promenade are like tall, thin ladies with blown-out hands and heads. Twice a day — or sometimes once during the day and once during the night — the tide comes creeping in.

At the large bay window in what is, I suppose, the drawing-room, there are thin, net curtains. From their hems grow orange-coloured tulips with dark brown leaves. They are a nice change. We don't need these shy curtains at home, as there is nobody to stare in the windows. Jane's first act was to twist one of them slyly in her hand, round and round, until she tore it from its foundations. Peg has taken it down and stitched the net together, but in the evening light the curtain seems to have a dark brown line across it, which anyhow matches the tulip leaves — though these, to a critical eye, look as if they came from a holly tree.

Morecambe is certainly not what it was thirty-five years ago. It is now a large and prosperous town, and I haven't seen any beggars in it yet. But it is still only June, a cold, blustery June so far. On the windiest Sunday, when we had taken the car up to Middleton Sands, Nicholas went up for his first trip in an aeroplane. When he came down, his eyes shone like diamonds with joy. He has wanted to go ever since he saw the first speck in the air that wasn't a bird. I know I must stay on the ground, and that the air doesn't want me, but I wouldn't stand in the way of anybody who wanted to go.

Jane is very small, yet. When my husband and Nicholas and my sister were rushing through the air in that frail bit of wood and canvas, she said in a troubled way to me that she didn't want daddy to be in that aeroplane (which she still mispronounces ullaplane in spite of all our efforts). Who, she asked, would drive the car? Despite her doleful words, the family came safely down, and the three of them ran grinning over the sands, looking so ecstatically happy that I felt for ever cut off from some sort of joy.

And now Nicholas has made his first religious — or anti-religious — announcement. He said, 'I don't believe there's a god, really.' I said 'Don't you?' in some perplexity; then quite truthfully but sadly, 'I do. I feel as if we wouldn't be here without something having thought of us in the first place'. Then he said, 'Perhaps we're only like toys to God, with our little fields, and our little roads, and our little motor-cars'. Yes, it is easy to see that he is a normal child who has been up in an aeroplane.

The first thing I did when I got to Morecambe was to buy an old copy of *East Lynne* and read it. I must have read it here as a child. And the same feeling surged up from the past and accompanied me. I had to read it in the same shamed manner, and it affected me in the same way. Yes, I howled once more over Little Willie. And then I read the *Diary of a Country Priest*, but that was all permeated with an *East Lynne* flavour. Physical and mental suffering was in it, and the appeal to the universe for one reason or another. Tonight, I don't want to appeal to the universe for anything. The tide comes in and goes out without my assistance. A hand can be put in the sea, but there are no statistics to show whether the particular drops of water it has once touched will ever be touched again by that hand. We have a faint idea of what happens to water, but we haven't really grasped what happens to the hand.

We have had baby's third birthday here. I got her a cake with three candles on it, and Birthday Greetings to Jane, and also a boat that can go on land or sea. Peg bought her a teddy bear with pale blue corduroy trousers on — are naked teddies fashionable no longer, or is something coy happening to the next generation? Days on earth often start so well that one feels a storm will blow up. Nick started a storm this day.

'This *lucky* baby,' he said. 'She's having a birthday in Morecambe, and I had to have mine at home!'

Nicholas is a jealous child, but having read the daily papers for years, we ought to know how to deal with this problem. The jealous child, we are told, has to be treated with a mixture of firm jollity and strong-minded impartiality. The authors of the articles forget that he wouldn't part with his jealousy for all the wealth of the Indies. It brings a child a lot of attention that he wouldn't get otherwise. Everybody sympathizes with the jealous child, and, remembering some part of their own unhappy youth, go out of their way to do him some favour. So his lot, on the whole, is a pleasant one. I am often much sorrier for poor Jane, who hasn't a dram of jealousy in her composition, than for my son. Yet the child problem in a flat can become acute; and little girls yell much more loudly and unreasonably than seven-year-old boys. So after three weeks, I have sent Peg and baby back home for a week or so, and Nick and I are staying here alone.

We can do as we like! But in a burst of wildest extravagance, I have already spent by Tuesday night the money that was to have kept us going to the end of the week. We have eight shillings left. That means just over half a crown a day to feed and amuse us. Once I should have thought it paradise to know that I had eight shillings. Now, I don't know what to do with it. The landlady, who lives on the premises, would cash a cheque; but I don't want that. We will organize our food and amusements so that they work out at this. Things arrive at home without having to be paid for, and everybody for miles around trusts us, sometimes, I think, too much — we have such a good reputation — so I forget that things are not the same here. The milk woman and the newspaper woman trust us, but perhaps nobody else would. So I look at the grey and green and black sky of an evening which hardly fades before another June morning dawns, and wonder just how much we shall get tomorrow for half a crown.

And then, after I had made this resolution, I cashed a cheque. I might die, I thought, with some money unspent.

The rain keeps on pouring down, a thick mist covers up the Cumberland hills, and the sea creeps in and out, soundlessly. But Nick and I don't mind anything, for we have found the pierrots. I often think of pierrots with solemn astonishment. They are the young who never grow old, and use their spirit of youth to make other people forget the dirty miseries of this earth.

The pier we frequent is the one I have known all my life, the pavilion of it was burned down one windy January long ago, and never rebuilt. There are little stuffy 'pill-boxes' lining the sides, in which old people sit and watch the waves, which fascinate my son as they once fascinated me. It costs threepence to walk upon these pieces of old wood which constitute the pier, and only threepence more to pass through the turnstile and enter what can really be thought of as a palace of varieties.

Nick and I went in, and the boy headed for the front row. He likes to see and hear everything. As I like to see and hear everything too, I followed him. It was an icy June day, with wind blowing through the cracks in the floorboards and twisting around until it even managed to get down necks and into earholes. A page-boy in a purple suit with silver buttons sold us what he called a 'lucky programme' for twopence. It had a number written on it in blue pencil. An attendant looked in with a trayful of ices, gave one glance at the blue noses of the audience and went back for hot coffee, which she retailed at threepence a cup.

Most of this enclosed area is open to the sky, but down one side, there is a few yards of roofing. Underneath this canopy, a cheerful lot of people were sitting. A good-looking but rather sad-faced young man in flannels came on the stage and arranged some music on the piano, and went behind the scenes. By and by, he came back in a shining black pierrot suit with pompoms, a green ruff round his neck, and a black handkerchief tied pirate-like about his head. He played a rousing opening chorus, without preliminaries. Nick nearly jumped out of his seat with joy. 'It's beginning!' he cried. It was his first pierrot show.

Four pierrots and three pierrettes dressed in black and green came from behind a curtain, singing at the top of their voices. They tripped to the extreme edge of the stage. There was no doubt we were going to see and hear everything.

From that moment, we were caught up and entranced by these people. The jokes were not new — I had heard some of them as a child on that very pier — but they seemed new, and we laughed aloud and applauded heartily. The comedian's speciality was being able to cry like a child. How could he help it? For though his hair was greying, he *was* a child, an eternal one. And the bills said that the show was 'under the direction' of this man, whatever that might mean. Each time he yelled, and put his hand over his eyes, and leaned against a supporting pillar, the audience yelled the louder with laughing. All the troubles they had had with their own children, the exasperation, the misunderstandings, were dissolved and made into something different by this man, something funny and to be borne.

The only time I want to be a painter is when I see people lost to themselves and to self-consciousness. I want to paint them then, when they are for once not acting, when their faces are good and innocent and empty and receptive as God probably intended them to be — and as Christ perhaps saw them. But I only got glimpses of that audience, for I myself was lost.

There was a round number called 'If I were not on the stage' that went with a great swing. Each artist threw himself into it, singing with gusto of what he would do. One would grind knives and scissors, another would be a showman, one a laundrywoman, one a barmaid. 'Mild and bitter, mild and bitter, four-pence to pay,' she would sing, pulling a beer-pump with her right hand, and holding out her left for an imaginary fourpence. Already in four days it is growing into a request number. The pierrots give three performances a day, whatever the weather. Nicholas and I go only to one, but we have yet to see anything repeated. This company is full of vitality.

Each one comes on the stage and gives the best of himself; and the more one gives of that sort of thing, the more seems to be born. The pierrettes are sensible and kindly-looking off stage, and quite beautiful on. The men — all five of them including the pianist — can be so funny that it hurts. The 'straight' singer — the best looking of them all — doesn't mind pulling his handsome face into any shape.

Towards the end of the performance, it came out that each programme was numbered, and that the person holding the 'lucky' number would get a prize — which turned out to be a bread-board. I am singularly unlucky in these things, so I knew the bread-board would never belong to me, though our own has just broken into two unequal pieces. A small boy was needed on the stage to draw a number out of a bag, and of course Nick went up. He was a great success, because when he is nervous, his Yorkshire accent comes out.

'A hoondred and sixty-five,' he told the comedian.

'Tell the audience,' said the comedian, laughing. '*We* can see it.'

He turned round fearlessly, 'A hoondred and sixty-five!' he shrieked.

As we were going out, the winner of the bread-board came up and pushed threepence into his hand. 'You did it very nicely,' she said. He has done it 'very nicely' three times since then, but though he looks round with the eyes of a hawk, no one else has tipped him.

After we had seen two or three performances, the straight singer jumped down from the stage to talk to us when the show was over. He told us that this was his first season 'outside', that he had always been 'in' before, that he was at the Floral Pavilion in New Brighton last year, and that he had had two seasons at Bournemouth. His eyes glowed when he mentioned Bournemouth.

I didn't like Bournemouth. It was always sandy and windy when I was there, so that I was glad to get away from it; and I had never been to New Brighton. So the conversation languished a little. I was outwardly shy and tongue-tied for the first time in years, as I am not used to handsome men, and I didn't know what to say. So for a diversion, he took Nick behind the scenes and the boy came out with red lips and pointed eyebrows daubed on.

The round-faced comedian bounded out in a light grey suit.

'You're not going to leave that on?' he said to me with some horror, looking at the child's decorations — though Nick was delighted with himself.

'*I* don't mind it,' I said.

'But everybody'll look at him,' he protested.

It seemed odd to me that this comedian, who wears a yellow velvet cap, with black bottles and spades printed on it, and has pink tights with dark brown cotton sewn on the calves to make it look as if his legs were hairy, and various other odd and out-of-the-way articles of dress, should worry over 'everybody' looking at the child. Nick and I have both a great deal of the mountebank in us. But the pointed eyebrows wouldn't wash off, even in the bath.

I have bought a lot of second-hand books, and one is all about a man's only child, and her upbringing. It is making me very sad. He seems to play with her most of the time, organized games, and treasure hunts — even pillow-fights — all those things which made me, when I encountered them as a child in other people's houses, quietly but desperately despise the grown-up world. He tells how he takes her to see a film with Charlie Chaplin in it, and after a time 'I heard her urgent whisper: "Daddy, may one laugh in here?"'

It is night now, and the long promenade lies quiet beneath its three-balled lights, and their reflections which shine from the wet concrete. And all the pierrots in this part of the world will soon be going to bed. Thirty years ago, my mother would go and listen to them. She got to know one called Lucy very well. Lucy was going to have a baby, yet she pranced about the stage in her short skirt and a hat made of chiffon, crying 'pretty pearls and *cet*'s eyes, some as big as *thet* size'. And one day in winter, she came to tea at our house, and cried, and mother said, 'Poor Lucy', and stroked her brown hair. For Lucy had got her baby, and her husband, who was a pierrot, too, was laid up by illness and without work, so Lucy was 'in panto-mime', and had to put her tiny baby out to nurse.

I am sorry the xylophone was ever invented. It was fun to get the miniature thing in a Christmas stocking, and bang away at it privately, but to enlarge the instru-ment until it has swelled out of all proportion, and then bang away at an audience is not, in my opinion, fair. I do not know whether this is common only of me, but I always hear two lots of notes where one is intended, so that I hear the tune played in two keys that do not match, one about five notes in the scale below the other.

At the weekend, my husband returned with Peg and the baby, and on Saturday night, he and I went to see another concert party. The only flaw in it was a xylo-phone, and that was played but once. The comedian of the show was a worried-looking man, who seemed to have moulded himself on Ford Sterling, that plastic-faced veteran of the silent cinema days. He told his 'feed' that he had eleven children. The other man said, 'What? Eleven children, and you only married two years?' 'It was a widow who proposed to me,' he said. 'Ooh, and I was sorry for her. She said she had ten little ones in the cemetery.' The feed said, 'Ten little ones in the cemetery? I should think you *were* sorry for her.' 'Yes,' said the comedian, 'but she forgot to say she'd only sent 'em there to play.'

And another time, he said he lived so far out in the country that the owls flirted with the chickens. This seemed to amuse the audience so much that it was a long time before he could resume.

But we liked the story of the old couple who decided to spend their golden wedding anniversary in the same hotel in which they spent their honeymoon. As they were getting ready for bed, the old woman grew sentimental. 'Do you remember,' she said, 'in this very room, on the first night we were married, you were so anxious to kiss me good-night that you hardly gave me time to get my stockings off.' 'Aye, lass,' said the old man. 'And you'd have time to *knit* a pair now.'

18

I have been prayed over by as many as three people at a time. What do they really want for me? I am possibly happier than most people, in that I can enjoy each day as it comes, and find something solemnly ludicrous in most situations. But the spate of prayer continues.

The farmer's wife had a long talk with me. It is possible that she prays most, for she says that I could be a power for good in the world if only I received 'The Word'. I said that if ever I did, and went about preaching it, I should only be thought mad. And she laughed and said yes, I should, but wasn't every prophet accounted mad? And she said, 'You'd be all right in yourself'.

Does that mean that religion is an armour against the sorrows of the world? I know very well that my disposition is joyful, on the top, and that I am satisfied with what happens to me. I should like the nice things that are given to me to be given to others; and I'd like to be able to take on the troubles of my fellow creatures. Because I bear trouble easily — or I think I do, which is the same thing.

I have deserted Morecambe for a few days — there is too much rain and too little sunshine this week — and come back to my empty house. Once again, the lawn is being scythed, but an older man is cutting the grass this July. Time himself has changed in a year. He was a youth then. Now he is an old man.

It is eerily lonely. The summer leaves shrivel under

fierce winds. No sunsets come to cheer the west windows, and the only shades of evening are pale grey, deep grey, and black. I am not afraid, but I lock the three doors each night, and I lock them whilst daylight is still with me. But when it is dark, and I am walking down the long passage to the kitchen, or when I cross the creaking upstairs landing, on to which any one of the seven dark doors may at any moment open, then sometimes I look behind me, and wonder if I shall see a horrible, inhuman face. One sometimes floats up from my childhood and haunts me. For once, a bearded stranger — already drunk at eleven o'clock on Sunday morning, and with bruised and swollen lips from which dribbled new blood over congealed blood — put his head in the door of our Sunday-school and asked for a pint. All the little scholars yelled and shrieked, and the man said apologetically, 'I thowt it were a pub'. As he propelled himself wavily away, some brave teacher rushed up and locked the door behind him, and we all stood yapping and whining, thinking that the devil had arrived to claim us. I was too young then to understand how funny it was. And all that got printed on my mind was a picture of that brutal, misunderstood, drunken visage, and it follows me down the years. There was contrition and sorrow in it, and even awe. The teachers said it was a horrible experience for us and them, but nobody ever said that it must have been a horrible experience for the poor wretch too.

Yesterday, I went to Leeds to see a friend. We had tea with her husband and two children. She likes eighteenth-century furniture, which is too plain and pure for me — I prefer an older and jollier oak, though I am quite content with mended pieces so long as they are smooth

143

and slippery and friendly — and has a lot of books arranged down a high wall in a way which always makes me think of a railway engine. She is tall, and her hair sticks out, and she writes impetuous stories and wears nice clothes, and is full of generosity and even fuller of scatter-brained plans than I am. She is always bringing me 'discoveries' which I found ten years ago, and then looking astonished but undismayed.

We were going out after tea, but a great thunderstorm gathered over Leeds and burst, so her husband put on a gramophone record which ran round and round, mimicking the thunderstorm as if it were a mouse behind a tiger. It was called 'The Love of the Three Oranges' March and Scherzo, by Prokofiev, and we had it on three times. In certain places, the husband made the gramophone sound louder, so that we laughed to hear the staccato cracks of the thunder followed by an echo from the record.

When we had got our enjoyment from that, he gave us Tchaikovsky's *Romeo and Juliet* music, on five records. I like to hear Tchaikovsky, and won't have him sneered at or damned without standing up for him. He has given me some pleasant, restful moments in my life. They let me choose next, and I chose César Franck's Symphony in D Minor, because I had always intended to hear it once. There is a lot of repetition in it — it seems like one of those very long books. But it served its purpose. And then, afterwards, I learned how one reads a score. I kept getting lost, as I do not know anything but tonic solfa, but it was exciting to follow the instruments. I have always been able to distinguish the different instruments in an orchestra, but did not realize until now that that was how a conductor conducted. If I grew deaf, I should learn to read musical scores properly, and for ever have an orchestra in my head.

For a long time, I had heard no music but that of dance bands, and César Franck became a little Agnes, pointing upwards. I wanted Bach. The only things I know at all by Bach are his G String Air and a very well-known Toccata and Fugue, intended for an organ, but much better liked by me played by a symphony orchestra. When I hear a kind of inspired rippling on an organ during a wireless programme which I switch on suddenly, I am quite aware that Bach fugues are being played, but I turn them off with a groan. I am living in a low world, and am not in a fit state for anything higher. I am like the man who 'thowt it were a pub', and I like my wireless to be a pub, though it is that but rarely. God bless the music-hall couple who come on to the rollicking tune of 'I love my wife, I love her *dearly*'.

I came back to Morecambe by car. It is a very nice run. We usually have lunch — if it is near lunchtime — at the Golden Lion, in Settle, but this day we set off late and grew hungry sooner, so we had it at the Maypole in Long Preston. The little waitress was pleasant, and smiled generously every time she brought us anything. She seemed eager to do her job properly and well. She said with breathless anxiety, 'What would you like for a sweet course, blackcurrant tart, or apple tart, or sponge pudding, or trifle?' I looked into her bright face, and said, 'What would *you* have?' and she said, 'Oh, *I'd* have the trifle!' So we had it, for I forgot the twenty-five years which probably lay between our ages. We should have had the blackcurrant tart, for blackcurrants are in season.

The way we are always welcomed by the children makes me understand why people who don't like children get dogs. I know there are people who like both dogs and children, but dogs are got by design. This welcoming business is touching. We are never away from the children for more than a day or two, but they are convinced that however good Peg is to them, the times when we are at home are better than the times we are not. And Peg is good to them, her Scotch strain goes by the board when she passes a toyshop window, and she spends most of her spare money on dolls and model aeroplanes for them. We have brought Nicholas a kite which is going to astonish the habitués of Middleton Sands tomorrow. It is large and full of colour, and there are parachutes with it. And baby has got a grand piano, about a foot long, with ten notes on it, which she plays unceasingly. Her eyes look as though somebody has handed her heaven on a platter.

Nick has made me a present tonight. It is his Saturday sixpence, unspent at seven o'clock, and delivered from a hot hand. I have taken it. He was out all afternoon, but would not spend anything. He resisted every temptation, to give this to me. And I think I know why. He did some shopping for Peg the other day, and coming back, lost the sixpence change. He couldn't resist going down to the beach on his way home, and it slipped through his fingers.

We were telling the people about it in the shop where he made his purchases. 'And we ran after him with the sixpence,' said the proprietress, laughing. 'It must have been meant for him to lose it. He'd made us some boats out of butter-paper, while he was waiting, with three cabins in'. She had kept one, and showed it to us. She laughed again, and said, 'And he said "If I get bored, I'll come and make you some more boats". But he never came back!'

I have put the sixpence on a shelf. I don't know that I should have given up my Saturday money — though it was only a penny in those days — because I had lost

146

some of my mother's money. Is this some meaning of the word 'Integrity'?

There's that inevitable thing about a tide coming in which might drive me crazy if I lived here for a long time. I should wish it to come over the promenade, and the gardens, and the housetops, just for a change. But it is orderly, and only the wildest storm could make it come even into the basements. The thunder never crashes loudly enough for me, and the sea is never wild enough. Storms go before I have had enough of them.

Now and again the truth has come so near to me that I see the shadow of its passing, and mourn. But God has not yet turned up. I can only conclude that I am not pure and upright, and that he is going to pass me by.

Well, that must be the way with many of us. I suppose I must lack understanding. So be it. My resolutions are first rate, but I don't often keep them. Baby wants to play with the back of my typewriter. Tears fill her eyes and run down her face when I gently detach her hands. I feel quite good-tempered this morning, so I stop to play with her, but she wants nothing beyond the back of the typewriter. And then, like St George, out of the everywhere into here, Nicholas lures her away to play with a toy motor.

Yes, my resolutions are often first rate. I should love to be able to stand on my own feet, without the doubts and hesitations I have now. I don't want to be safe in the arms of Jesus, because I should be restless to get out after a very short time — and even ashamed. I do not see the need of a heaven. I cannot say of the 'fire of life' that 'it sinks, and I am ready to depart', because I may be useful in a thousand ways yet; there may be more laughter and more tears, but surely they will both be mellower. But I do say that life has been perfect in parts, and that I am and always shall be grateful and glad that I was ever born.